LOST IN THE COSMOS

ALSO BY WALKER PERCY

NOVELS

THE MOVIEGOER (1961)

THE LAST GENTLEMAN (1966)

LOVE IN THE RUINS (1971)

LANCELOT (1977)

THE SECOND COMING (1980)

THE THANATOS SYNDROME (1987)

NONFICTION

THE MESSAGE IN THE BOTTLE (1975)

SIGNPOSTS IN A STRANGE LAND (1991)

LOST IN THE COSMOS

THE LAST SELF-HELP BOOK

WALKER PERCY

PICADOR

FARRAR, STRAUS AND GIROUX

NEW YORK

www.picadorusa.com

Picador® is a U.S. registered trademark and is used by Farrar, Straus and Giroux under license from Pan Books Limited.

For information on Picador Reading Group Guides, as well as ordering, please contact the Trade Marketing department at St. Martin's Press.
Phone: 1-800-221-7945 extension 763
Fax: 212-677-7456
E-mail: trademarketing@stmartins.com

ISBN 0-312-25399-0

First published in the United States by Farrar, Straus and Giroux

10 9 8 7

For my fellow space travelers,
John Walker, Robert, David, Jack

We are unknown, we knowers, to ourselves . . . Of necessity we remain strangers to ourselves, we understand ourselves not, in our selves we are bound to be mistaken, for each of us holds good to all eternity the motto, "Each is the farthest away from himself"—as far as ourselves are concerned we are not knowers.

NIETZSCHE

LOST IN THE COSMOS:
THE LAST SELF-HELP BOOK

or

The Strange Case of the Self, your Self, the Ghost which Haunts the Cosmos

or

How you can survive in the Cosmos about which you know more and more while knowing less and less about yourself, this despite 10,000 self-help books, 100,000 psychotherapists, and 100 million fundamentalist Christians

or

Why it is that of all the billions and billions of strange objects in the Cosmos—novas, quasars, pulsars, black holes—you are beyond doubt the strangest

or

Why it is possible to learn more in ten minutes about the Crab Nebula in Taurus, which is 6,000 light-years away, than you presently know about yourself, even though you've been stuck with yourself all your life

or

How it is possible for the man who designed Voyager 19, which arrived at Titania, a satellite of Uranus, three seconds off schedule and a hundred yards off course after a flight of six years, to be one of the most screwed-up creatures in California—or the Cosmos

plus

A Twenty-Question Quiz which will not help you become rich or more assertive or more creative or make love better but which may—though it probably won't, considering how useless self-help books generally are—help you discover who you are not and even—an outside chance—who you are

plus

A preliminary short quiz which you can take standing in a bookstore and which will allow you to determine whether you need to buy this book and proceed to the Twenty Questions

plus

A short history of the Cosmos, including a semiotic theory of the Self which explains why it is that man is the only alien creature, as far as we know, in the entire Cosmos

plus

A space odyssey which gives an account of what can happen to an earthling astronaut if there is somebody out there and what can happen if there is no one out there

A Preliminary Short Quiz
so that you may determine whether you need to take the
Twenty-Question Self-Help Quiz. If you can answer
these questions, you are not lost in the Cosmos

I imagine that you are reading a book about the Cosmos. You find it so interesting that you go out and buy a telescope. One fine clear moonless night you set up your telescope and focus on the brightest star in the sky. It is a planet, not a star, with a reddish spot and several moons. Excited, you look up the planets in your book about the Cosmos. You read a description of the planets. You read a sentence about a large yellowish planet with a red spot and several moons. You recognize both the description and the picture. Clearly, you have been looking at Jupiter.

You have no difficulty at all in saying that it is Jupiter, not Mars or Saturn, even though the object you are looking at is something you have never seen before and is hundreds of millions of miles distant.

Now imagine that you are reading the newspaper. You come to the astrology column. You may or may not believe in astrology, but to judge from the popularity of astrology these days, you will probably read your horoscope. According to a recent poll, more Americans set store in astrology than in science or God.

You are an Aries. You open your newspaper to the astrology column and read an analysis of the Aries personality. It says, among other things:

You have the knack of creating an atmosphere of thought and movement, unhampered by petty jealousies. But you have the tendency to scatter your talents to the four winds.

Hm, you say, quite true. I'm like that.

Suddenly you realize you've made a mistake. You've read the Gemini column. So you go back to Aries:

Nothing hurts you more than to be unjustly mistreated or suspected. But you have a way about you, a gift for seeing things through despite all obstacles and distractions. You also have a desperate need to be liked. So you have been wounded more often than you will admit.

Hm, you say, quite true. I'm like that.

The first question is: Why is it that both descriptions seem to fit you—or, for that matter, why do you seem to recognize yourself in the self-analysis of all twelve astrological signs? Or, to put it another way, why is it that you can recognize and identify the planets Jupiter and Venus so readily after reading a bit and taking one look, yet have so much trouble identifying yourself from twelve descriptions when, presumably, you know yourself much better than you know Jupiter and Venus?

(2) Can you explain why it is that there are, at last count, sixteen schools of psychotherapy with sixteen theories of the personality and its disorders and that patients treated in one school seem to do as well or as badly as patients treated in any other—while there is only one generally accepted theory of the cause and cure of pneumococcal pneumonia and only one generally accepted theory of the orbits of the planets and the gravitational attraction of our galaxy and the galaxy M31

in Andromeda? (Hint: If you answer that the human psyche is more complicated than the pneumococcus and the human white-cell response or the galaxies or Einstein's general theory of relativity, keep in mind that the burden of proof is on you. Or if you answer that the study of the human psyche is in its infancy, remember then this infancy has lasted 2,500 years and, unlike physics, we don't seem to know much more about the psyche than Plato did.)

(3) How do you explain these odd little everyday phenomena with which everyone is familiar:

You have seen yourself a thousand times in the mirror, face to face. No sight is more familiar. Yet why is it that the first time you see yourself in a clothier's triple mirror—from the side, so to speak—it comes as a shock? Or the first time you saw yourself in a home movie: were you embarrassed? What about the first time you heard your recorded voice—did you recognize it? Clearly, you should, since you've been hearing it all your life.

Why is it that, when you are shown a group photograph in which you are present, you always (and probably covertly) seek yourself out? To see what you look like? Don't you know what you look like?

Has this ever happened to you? You are walking along a street of stores. There are other people walking. You catch a glimpse in a store window of a reflection of a person. For a second or so you do not recognize the person. He, she, seems a total stranger. Then you realize it is your own reflection. Then in a kind of transformation, the reflection does in fact become your familiar self.

One of the peculiar ironies of being a human self in the Cosmos: A stranger approaching you in the street will in a second's glance see you whole, size you up, place you in a way in which you cannot and never will, even though you have spent a lifetime with yourself, live in the Century of the Self, and therefore ought to know yourself best of all.

The question is: Why is it that in your entire lifetime you will never be able to size yourself up as you can size up somebody else—or size up Saturn—in a ten-second look?

Why is it that the look of another person looking at you is different from everything else in the Cosmos? That is to say, looking at lions or tigers or Saturn or the Ring Nebula or at an owl or at another person from the side is one thing, but finding yourself looking into the eyes of another person looking at you is something else. And why is it that one can look at a lion or a planet or an owl or at someone's finger as long as one pleases, but looking into the eyes of another person is, if prolonged past a second, a perilous affair?

(4) The following experiment was performed on a group of ten subjects. See how you would answer the questions.

Think of five acquaintances, not close friends, not lovers, not family members.

Describe each by three adjectives (in the experiment, a "personality characteristic chart" was provided on which one could score an acquaintance on a scale of "good" and "bad" qualities, e.g., more or less trustworthy, attractive, boring, intelligent, selfish, flighty, outgoing, introspective, and so on). Thus, you might describe an acquaintance named Gary McPherson as fairly good company, moderately trustworthy, funny but a little malicious, and so on. Or Linda Ellison: fairly good-looking (a 7 or 7½), more intelligent than she lets on, a good listener. And so on.

Note that most if not all of your adjectives could be placed on a finite scale, say from a plus ten to a minus ten.

Now, having described five acquaintances, do the following. Read these two sentences carefully:

(*a*) You are extraordinarily generous, ecstatically loving of the right person, supremely knowledgeable about what is wrong with the country, about people, capable of moments of insight unsurpassed by any scientist or artist or writer in the country. You possess an infinite potentiality.

(*b*) You are of all people in the world probably the most selfish, hateful, envious (e.g., you take pleasure in reading death notices in the newspaper and in hearing of an acquaintance's heart attack), the most treacherous, the most frightened, and above all the phoniest.

Now answer this question as honestly as you can: Which of these two sentences more nearly describes you? CHECK (*a*), (*b*), (neither), (both).

If you checked (both)—60 percent of respondents did— how can that be?

(5) Do you understand sexuality?

That is to say, are you happy with either of the two standard versions of sexuality:

One, the biological—that the sex drive is one among several needs and drives evolved through natural selection as a means of sustaining the life of the organism and ensuring the survival of the species. Thus, sexual desire is one item on a list which includes other such items as hunger, thirst, needs of shelter, nest-building, migration, and so on.

The other, the religious-humanistic—sex is an expression, perhaps the ultimate expression, of love and communication between a man and a woman, and is best exemplified in marriage, raising children, the sharing of a life, family, home, and fireside.

Or do you see sexuality as a unique trait of the present-day self (which is the only self we know), occupying an absolutely central locus in the consciousness particularly as it relates to other sexual beings, of an order and magnitude of power incommensurate with other "drives" and also specified by the very structure of the present-day self as its very core and as its prime avenue of intercourse with others?

If the sexual drive is but one of several biological needs, why are we living in the most eroticized society in history? Why don't TV, films, billboards, magazines feature culinary delights, e.g., huge chocolate cakes, hams, roasts, strawberries, instead of women's bodies?

Or are you more confused about sexuality than any other phenomenon in the Cosmos?

Do you know why it is that men and women exhibit sexual behavior undreamed of among the other several million species, with every conceivable sexual relation between persons, or with only one person, or between a male and female, or between two male persons, or two female persons, or two males and one female, or two females and one male; relationships moreover which can implicate every orifice and appendage of the human body and which bear no relation to the reproduction and survival of the species?

Is the following statement true or false:

Pornography is not an aberration of a few sexually frustrated middle-aged men in gray raincoats; it is rather a salient and prime property of modern consciousness, of three hundred years of technology and the industrial revolution, and is symptomatic of a radical disorder in the relation of the self to other selves which generally manifests itself in the abstracted state of one self (male) and the degradation of another self (female) to an abstract object of satisfaction.

(6) Consider the following short descriptions of different kinds of consciousness of self. Which of the selves, if any, do you identify with?

(*a*) *The cosmological self.* The self is either unconscious of itself or only conscious of itself insofar as it is identified with a cosmological myth or classificatory system, e.g., totemism. Ask a Bororo tribesman: Who are you? He may reply: I am parakeet. (Ask an L.S.U. fan at a football game: Who are you? He may reply: I am a tiger.)

(*b*) *The Brahmin-Buddhist self.* Who are you? What is your self? My self in this life is impaled on the wheel of nonbeing, obscured by the veil of unreality. But it can realize itself by penetrating the veil of *maya* and plumbing the depths of self until it achieves *nirvana*, nothingness, or the *Brahman*, God. The *atman* (self) is the *Brahman* (God).

(*c*) *The Christian self (and, to a degree, the Judaic and Islamic self).* The self sees itself as a creature, created by God, estranged from God by an aboriginal catastrophe, and now reconciled with him. Before the reconciliation, the self is, as Paul told the Ephesians, a stranger to every covenant, with no promise to hope for, with the world about you and no God. But now the self becomes a son of God, a member of a family of selves, and is conscious of itself as a creature of God embarked upon a pilgrimage in this life and destined for happiness and reunion with God in a later life.

(*d*) *The role-taking self.* One sociological view of the self is that the self achieves its identity by taking roles and modeling its own role from the roles of others, e.g., one's mother, father, housewife, breadwinner, macho-boy-man, feminine-doll-girl, etc.—and also, as George Meade said, upon how one perceives others' perceptions of oneself.

*(e) The standard American-Jeffersonian high-school-com-
mencement Republican-and-Democratic-platform self.* The
self is an individual entity created by God and endowed with
certain inalienable rights and the freedom to pursue happiness
and fulfill its potential. It achieves itself through work, participation in society, family, the marketplace, the political
process, cultural activities, sports, the sciences, and the arts.
It follows that in a free and affluent society the self should
succeed more often than not in fulfilling itself. Happiness
can be pursued and to a degree caught.

(f) The diverted self. In a free and affluent society, the
self is free to divert itself endlessly from itself. It works in
order to enjoy the diversions that the fruit of one's labor can
purchase. The pursuit of happiness becomes the pursuit of
diversion, and in this society the possibilities of diversion are
endless and as readily available as eight hours of television a
day: TV, sports, travel, drugs, games, newspapers, magazines,
Vegas.

(g) The lost self. With the passing of the cosmological
myths and the fading of Christianity as a guarantor of the
identity of the self, the self becomes dislocated, Jefferson or
no Jefferson, is both cut loose and imprisoned by its own
freedom, yet imprisoned by a curious and paradoxical bondage
like a Chinese handcuff, so that the very attempts to free
itself, e.g., by ever more refined techniques for the pursuit of
happiness, only tighten the bondage and distance the self ever
farther from the very world it wishes to inhabit as its home-
land. The rational Jeffersonian pursuit of happiness embarked
upon in the American Revolution translates into the flaky
euphoria of the late twentieth century. Every advance in an
objective understanding of the Cosmos and in its technological
control further distances the self from the Cosmos precisely
in the degree of the advance—so that in the end the self be-

comes a space-bound ghost which roams the very Cosmos it understands perfectly.

(*h*) *The scientific and artistic self.* Or that self which is so totally absorbed in the pursuit of art or science as to be self-less. The modern caricature is the "absentminded professor" or the demonic possessed artist, which is to say that as a self he is "absent" from the usual concerns of the self about itself in the world. E.g., Karl von Frisch and his bees, Schubert in a beer hall writing lieder on the tablecloth, Picasso in a restaurant modeling animals from bread.

(*i*) *The illusory self.* Or the conviction that one's sense of oneself is a psychological or cultural illusion and that with the advance of science, e.g., behaviorism, Lévi-Strauss's structuralism, the self will disappear.

(*j*) *The autonomous self.* The self sees itself as a sovereign and individual consciousness, liberated by education from the traditional bonds of religion, by democracy from the strictures of class, by technology from the drudgery of poverty, and by self-knowledge from the tyranny of the unconscious—and therefore free to pursue its own destiny without God.

(*k*) *The totalitarian self.* The self sees itself as a creature of the state, fascist or communist, and understands its need to be specified by the needs of the state.

(CHECK ONE)

If you can answer Questions (1) through (5) and did not check (6g), you probably do not need to take the Twenty-Question Quiz.

Twenty-Question Multiple-Choice Self-Help Quiz
to test your knowledge of the peculiar status of the self,
your self and other selves, in the Cosmos, and your knowledge of what to do with your self in these, the last years
of the twentieth century

(1) THE AMNESIC SELF: *Why the Self Wants to Get Rid of Itself*

In all soap operas and in many films and novels, a leading character will sooner or later develop amnesia. He will not necessarily develop pneumonia or cancer or schizophrenia, but inevitably he will be overtaken by amnesia. He (or she) finds himself in a strange place, having forgotten his old place, his family, friends, business. He begins a new life in a new place with a new girlfriend, new job. After a while in his new life he begins to receive clues about his old life. A stranger stops him in the street and calls him by a strange name. The best exploitation of the pleasures of amnesia occurred in Hitchcock's *Spellbound* where Gregory Peck had amnesia and Ingrid Bergman was his psychiatrist. For the moviegoer there occurred first the pleasure of the prospect of a new life and the infinite possibilities of the self as represented by Gregory Peck. The second pleasure is the accidental meeting with Ingrid Bergman, who is sensitive to the clues that Gregory misses, and who is a reliable guide, his Beatrice, who can help him recover his old life—for even amnesia, if prolonged, can become as dreary as one's old life.

Here is a nice example of Ingrid picking up clues to his past identity, a search which will allow them to have the best of both worlds, a discovery of oneself and one's past without the encumbrances of the past, and a joining of hands with Ingrid for a new life in the future:

INGRID (*psychoanalyzing him in a hotel room*): I would like to ask you a medical question.

GREGORY: All right.

INGRID: How would you diagnose a pain in the right upper quadrant?

GREGORY: Gall bladder—pneumonia—

INGRID: It is obvious you are a doctor.

Here is an extra dividend for the moviegoer who is identifying with Peck or Bergman. Ingrid is on the track of who he is (who you are). You are a doctor, an identity which seems to interest women more than, say, a banker or an auto dealer.

Question: Is amnesia a favorite device in fiction and especially soap operas because

(*a*) The character in the soap opera is sick and tired of himself and his life and wants a change.

(*b*) The writer is sick and tired of his character and wants a change.

(*c*) The writer is sick and tired of himself and his life and wants a change.

(*d*) The reader or moviegoer or TV-viewer is sick and tired of himself and his life and wants a change—and the housewife is the sickest and tiredest of all.

(*e*) The times are such that everyday life for everybody is more or less intolerable and one is better off wiping out the past and starting anew.

(CHECK ONE)

A variant of the amnesic-plot device is the inadvertent return of the amnesiac to home territory, where he is welcomed by a lovely woman, unknown to him, who is evidently his wife. The crucial scene is his being led off to bed.

A non-amnesic equivalent is a twin or look-alike who is mistaken for someone else—by a beautiful woman. Invariably she finds him not merely oddly different but somehow better, more attractive, than the original. After a love scene, she looks at him wide-eyed and smiling (you were never like this before!).

This version demonstrates that the source of pleasure for the moviegoer is not the amnesia but the certified and risk-free license to leave the old self behind and enter upon a new life, whether by amnesia or mistaken identity.

Thought Experiment: Test your response to vicarious loss of self by imagining amnesia raised to the highest power. Imagine a soap opera in which a character awakens every morning with amnesia, in a strange house with a strange attractive man (or woman), welcomed by the stranger, looking out a strange window with a strange view, having forgotten the past each morning and starting life afresh, seeing the window, the view, himself, herself, in the mirror afresh and for the first time. Does this prospect intrigue you? If it does, what does this say about your non-amnesic self?*

---

* Some TV series do in fact operate at this level of amnesia, the doctor or cop or private eye falling in love every week, the lover totally forgotten the following week. This quasi-amnesic device is clearly a variant of the earlier Lone Ranger or non-amnesic Western, with the difference that in the latter the lone cowboy moves on after his adventure, whereas in the former it is the lover who moves on.

(2) THE SELF AS NOUGHT: *How the Self Tries to Inform Itself by Possessing Things which do not Look like the Things They're Used as*

In a recent issue of a home-and-garden magazine, an article listed fifty ways to make a coffee table.

One table was made of an old transom of stained glass supported by an antique brass chandelier cut ingeniously to make the legs.

Another was a cypress stump, waxed and highly polished.

Another was a big spool used for telephone cable set on end.

Another was a lobster trap.

Another was a Coca-Cola sign propped on Coke crates.

Another was a stone slab from an old morgue, the blood runnel used as an ash tray.

Another was a hayloft door set on cut-down sawhorses.

Another was the hatch of a sailboat mounted on halves of ships' wheels.

Another was a cobbler's bench.*

Not a single one was a table designed as such, that is, a horizontal member with four legs.

---

* Yet another article (*The New York Times*, September 3, 1981) listed the following objects which were offered for *sale* and specifically for *use* as coffee tables: walnut clock ($2,200), ventilator duct grills ($300), sandstone mask ($250), Ionic column capital ($400), Nigerian chieftain's stool ($2,500), nineteenth-century English camphor chest ($2,350), trundle pine storage box ($550), nineteenth-century Norman poultry cage ($450), Korean coin chest ($350), fiberboard musical-instrument case ($175), Chinese bamboo trunk ($50).

Question: Why was not a single table designed as such rather than being a non-table doing duty as a table?

(*a*) Because people have gotten tired of ordinary tables.

(*b*) Because the fifty non-tables converted to use as tables make good conversation pieces.

(*c*) Because it is a chance to make use of valuable odds and ends which otherwise would gather dust in the attic.

(*d*) Because the self in the twentieth century is a voracious nought which expands like the feeding vacuole of an amoeba seeking to nourish and inform its own nothingness by ingesting new objects in the world but, like a vacuole, only succeeds in emptying them out.

(CHECK ONE)

Thus, ordinary four-legged tables have long since been emptied out and rendered invisible.

Even the cobbler's bench, which, for a while, resisted the ravenous self and for some years remained a cobbler's bench upon which one could set drinks and art books, has now disappeared into the vacuole and become as invisible as a Danish modern. The cobbler's bench has become in fact a table. Tables are now being manufactured which look like cobbler's benches but are not.

Thought Experiment: Try to imagine the circumstances under which the fifty non-tables converted to use as coffee tables would become less and less desirable until one would actually prefer an ordinary table constructed of four legs and a top. E.g., imagine you are an archeologist of the twenty-first century, exploring the abandoned beach cottages of Martha's Vineyard and finding all manner of strange artifacts used as tables—pieces of driftwood, capstans, shark jaws—and that you need a good worktable and, not recognizing these objects as tables, you construct a simple and sturdy table from a plank of wood and four lengths of two-by-fours.

Thought Experiment (II): Consider to what extent an "antique" is prized because it is excellently made and beautiful and to what extent it is prized because it is an antique and as such is saturated with another time and another place and is therefore resistant to absorption by the self—just as a pine piling saturated in creosote resists corrosion by the sea—and thus possesses a higher coefficient of informing power for the nought of self.

If you say that a writing table made by Thomas Sheraton is of value because it is excellently made and beautiful, how would you go about making a writing table now that would be similarly prized as an antique two hundred years from now?

The real question of course is whether the twentieth-century self is different from the eighteenth-century self, both in its reliance on "antiques" to inform itself and in its ability to make a writing table which is graceful and useful and for no other reason. Was a well-to-do eighteenth-century Englishman content to buy a Sheraton writing table, or would he have preferred a fifteenth-century "antique"?

THE SELF AS NOUGHT (II): *Why Most Women, and Some Men, are Subject to Fashion*

There is no fashion so absurd, even grotesque, that it cannot be adopted, given two things: the authority of the fashion-setter (Dior, Jackie Onassis) and the vacuity or noughtness of the consumer. E.g., bustles in the West, bound feet in the East.

It happens that a woman will see a new fashion, a certain kind of hat, a new hairstyle, the cut and length of a skirt, a French-wrap swimsuit, and she will want it. She buys it. Often the source of the fashion is a famous and attractive person or a well-known couturier.

It is illuminating that some fashions are set by mistake. It is reported, for example, that when Wallis Warfield Simpson appeared at Ascot with the second button of her blouse left inadvertently unbuttoned, millions of women followed suit. And when John Wayne's belt buckle slipped to one side in a scene in the movie *Red River*, thousands of urban cowboys began to buckle their belts to the side.

In a certain New York disco located near a hospital, interns and nurses would drop in at all hours wearing their hospital greens. Whereupon it became fashionable for non-medical people to go discoing in wrinkled hospital greens—which are now sold at J. C. Penney.*

---

* This efficacy of fashion-by-mistake is similar to metaphor-by-mistake—those instances when a word misread is better than the word intended, like the ordinary belt doing its ordinary duty holding up pants being perceived as not as desirable as a belt with buckle worn to the side. Consider Empson's example of metaphor-by-mistake:

The efficacy of fashion turns on the self's perception of itself either as a nought or at least as lacking something, and its perception or misperception of the splendid wholeness of public figures as evidenced by even the most carelessly worn badges of their substantiality—when in truth the selves of Jackie Onassis and Wallis Simpson and John Wayne are probably more insubstantial than most.

Question: What does the saleslady mean when she fits a customer with an article of clothing and says: "It's you"?

(*a*) She means the same thing the customer means if you should ask her: It is becoming to me. It looks nice. I don't have a thing to wear.* It does something for me.

(*b*) She means that it—the hat, blouse, hairstyle, dress— actually accentuates your best features—eyes, hair—while minimizing your worst: no neck, etc.

(*c*) It will please your husband or lover.

(*d*) It will impress other women.

(*e*) Most other women are already wearing it and you look dowdy without it.

(*f*) The saleslady means what she says. It really *is* you. That is, you are not much without it, you perceive yourself as mousy, and you are a something—your self in fact, your new true self—with it.

(CHECK ONE)

Queenlily June with a rose in her hair
Moves to her prime with a languorous air

Nice lines—because he misread Queenlily as Queen Lily, when the poet had only intended the adverb of queenly.

* What does a woman mean when she says "I don't have a thing to wear," when in fact she has a closet full of clothes? While her statement seems absurd to her husband or a connivance to get more clothes, she is telling the truth. She does not have a *thing* to wear because all the things hanging in her closet have been emptied out and become invisible.

She might as justifiably reply to him: "Why do you need a new car? This one works perfectly well."

But if the saleslady means what she says—and since you have gone through any number of such styles in the past—then it must follow that the other articles in the past were also you and are no longer. How can that be? It could only be because some sort of consumption takes place. The nought which is you has devoured the style and been sustained for a while as a non-you until the style is emptied out by the noughting self.

Consider the stages of the consumption:

First stage: You see an article or a style worn by a person with a certain authority. At first glance it seems outlandish, even absurd. Or ugly, like the long skirt of the New Look of the 1950s.

Second stage: You see more people wearing it. It is still outlandish, but it is an outlandish *something* and you are fading.

Third stage: You try it on. The saleslady says it is you. You laugh, shrug, shake your head, but secretly the possibility is born that it *can* be you.

Fourth stage: You buy it and wear it. For a while, it *is* you and you are it. That is, you perceive it as informing you and you as informed, either as a new you or the old real you which has never come to light before.

Fifth stage: Gradually the new style becomes everyday, quotidian, rendered neutral. No matter how exotic it is, like a morsel to which an amoeba is attracted and which it surrounds and takes into itself, it is devoured and becomes part of the transparent flowing substance of the amoeba.

Sixth stage: After a sufficient lapse of time, the husk or residue of the new style is excreted and becomes an oddity, a slightly shameful thing but still attached, like the waste in the excretory vacuole of the amoeba.

If you don't believe this, take a look at an old snapshot of yourself wearing a Jackie-O pillbox hat twenty years ago—

or a ducktail Elvis haircut. You will laugh or frown and put
it away. It looks queer. It is not only not you. It is a not-you.

Thought Experiment: Assuming there is a certain perceived,
or misperceived, authority behind the setting of a fashion,
e.g., the attractiveness and fame of a Jackie O, John Wayne,
or the putative knowledgeability of Dior, try to imagine the
nature of the authority of the fashion-setter and the state of
mind of the consumer which brought it to pass that women
wore *bustles*, which made their rear ends grotesquely prominent when women's rear ends are already more prominent,
relatively speaking, than any other mammal's.

(3) THE NOWHERE SELF: *How the Self, Which Usually Experiences Itself as Living Nowhere, is Surprised to Find that it Lives Somewhere*

On the Johnny Carson Show, it always happens that when Carson or one of his guests mentions the name of an American city, there is applause from those audience members who live in this city. The applause is of a particular character, startled and immediate, as if the applauders cannot help themselves.

Such a response is understandable if one hails from a hamlet like Abita Springs, Louisiana, and Carson mentioned Abita Springs. But the applause also occurs at the mention of New York or Chicago.

Question: Do Chicagoans in Burbank, California, applaud at the mention of the word Chicago

(*a*) Because they are proud of Chicago?

(*b*) Because they are boosters, Chamber of Commerce types, who appreciate a plug, much as a toothpaste manufacturer would appreciate Carson mentioning Colgate?

(*c*) Because a person, particularly a passive audience member who finds himself in Burbank, California, feels himself so dislocated, so detached from a particular coordinate in space and time, so ghostly, that the very mention of such a coordinate is enough to startle him into action?

(CHECK ONE)

Thought Experiment: You are a native of New York City, you live in New York, work in New York, travel about the city with no particular emotion except a mild boredom, unease, exasperation, and a dislike especially for, say, Times Square and Brooklyn, and a longing for a Connecticut farmhouse. You make enough money and move to a Connecticut farmhouse. Later you become an astronaut and wander in space for years. You land on a strange, unexplored (you think) planet. There you find a road sign with an arrow, erected by a previous astronaut in the manner of GIs in World War II: "Brooklyn 9.6 light-years." Explain your emotion.

(4) THE FEARFUL SELF: *Why the Self is so Afraid of Being Found Out*

A recent poll asked people what they feared most. A majority of respondents agreed in ranking one fear above all others, above fear of sickness, accidents, crime, war, even death. It is the fear of speaking before a group, stage fright.

Yet, in the conventional objective scientific view, man is an organism among other organisms and a man should therefore not be terrified to be surrounded by his own kind, other like organisms who are not merely not hostile but by the very nature of the occasion well disposed, and to open his mouth and speak in a language he has learned from his fellowmen. A wolf howling alone in a wolfpack doesn't get stage fright.

Question: What is so frightening to so many people about speaking to an audience?

(*a*) Is it because the ever-present chance of making a fool of oneself before one person is multiplied by the number of listeners, so that an audience of 50 persons is 50 times more terrifying than one? Is an audience of 50 million a million times more terrifying than 50?

(*b*) Is it because, since one person, friend or stranger, is often difficult to deal with, 50 people are 50 times more difficult?

(*c*) Is it because, say with an audience of 500, you are being looked at by at least 499 people whose gaze you cannot defend against by looking back, that is, you are being seen from this or that vulnerable angle where your mask or persona may not be in place?

(d) Is it because you fear a total failure of performance such as never happened in the history of the world, so that not one word will come to your mind and world chaos will follow? As evidence of such a danger, note the uneasiness of a playgoing audience when an actor forgets his lines or a congregation when a preacher falls silent for no apparent reason. The escalating terror of such a silence is a public phenomenon: five seconds of such silence is a very long time, ten seconds is almost intolerable.

(e) Is it because you know that what you present to the world is a persona, a mask, that it is a very fragile disguise, that God alone knows what is underneath since you clearly do not, perhaps nothing less than the self itself, and that if the persona fails, what is revealed is unspeakable (literally, because you can't speak it), like what was revealed when the Phantom of the Opera had his mask ripped off, a no-face, a vacancy, a hole which is much worse than the ugliest face—so frightening, in fact, that you remember, as a child, crawling under the seat in the movie?

Thought Experiment: If you are a shy person, which of the following situations is the most terrifying to you? Which is the least terrifying?

In the first, you are a mid-echelon executive in the sales division of a large company in which you are both successful and well liked. You are scheduled to deliver a speech at the annual banquet, an honor. You have months to prepare.

In the second, you are the character Richard Hannay in Hitchcock's *The Thirty-nine Steps.* Pursued down a street by his enemies, he ducks into a doorway which happens to be a stage door and finds himself on stage at a political rally where he is mistaken for the guest speaker and introduced. He has not the faintest idea what he is supposed to talk about.

In the third, the world's population has been destroyed by nuclear wars. Only you have survived. The earth is invaded by extraterrestrial beings. They capture you and haul you up before a large tribunal and make it known to you that you must give an account of yourself, what you are doing here, why you should be spared, etc.

Explain your choice.

Thought Experiment (II): Explain why Moses was tongue-tied and stagestruck before his fellow Jews but had no trouble talking to God.

Explain on what grounds Christ told his followers not to worry if they were arrested and required to testify before a court of their enemies. You will know what to say, he told them. Did he imply that it is easier to talk to enemies than to friends and that the real problem arises when one is required to address one's fellow Christians in the church at Corinth?

(5) The Fearful Self (II): *Why the Self is so Afraid of being Stuck with another Self*

Johnny Carson, when questioned about his aplomb on the stage before a TV audience of millions, replied: Sure, I'm at ease up here—because I'm in control—but when I'm at a cocktail party and caught in a one-on-one conversation: panic city!

Question: What do Johnny Carson and other shy people fear when they are caught in a "one-on-one" conversation at a cocktail party? That is, what is the worst case, the worst thing that can happen?

(*a*) That you can't think of anything interesting to say and the other person will be bored?

(*b*) That the other person has nothing to say that you want to hear and you know you will be bored?

(*c*) That neither of you has anything to say and therefore the world will come to an end, or rather, something worse than the end of the world, or, as Carson would say, panic city—that is, a predicament in which all options open to you are more intolerable than the end of the world?

(*d*) That there are only two means of escape, both of which are intolerable: either you leave, which will hurt the other person's feelings, or the other person leaves, which will hurt your feelings?

(*e*) That you will be exposed, that is, that the unique unformulability, the singular nought, which you secretly believe yourself to be, will be exposed at last, the one black hole among a billion other ordinary stars?

(CHECK ONE)

Thought Experiment: Imagine that you are Johnny Carson and find yourself caught in an intolerable one-on-one conversation at a cocktail party from which there is no escape.

Which of the two following events would you prefer to take place: (1) That the other person become more and more witty and charming, the music more beautiful, the scene transformed to a villa at Capri on the loveliest night of the year, while you find yourself more and more at a loss; or (2) that you are still in Beverly Hills and the chandeliers begin to rattle, a 7.5 Richter earthquake takes place, and presently you find yourself and the other person alive and well, and talking under a mound of rubble.

If your choice is (2), explain why it is possible for a true conversation to take place under the conditions of (2) but not (1).

(6) THE FEARFUL SELF (III): *How the Self Tries to Escape its Predicament*

Question: If you are a shy person, is it better to accept your shyness, or to seek help from a psychotherapist in order to become an assertive outgoing person, or perhaps to read a book about overcoming shyness?

(*a*) It is better to seek help from a psychotherapist because it is better not to suffer than to suffer. Psychiatrists and psychologists treat disorders. Shyness is a symptom of such a disorder. Therefore, it is reasonable to seek such help.

(*b*) It is better to read a book about how to get over being shy, anxious, insecure, and so on, than not to read such a book, because one might learn a helpful thing or two, even from a book.

(*c*) It is better not to read such a book because the effects of such books last only during the reading of the book and perhaps fifteen minutes after finishing it, and therefore your despair is only increased.

(*d*) It is better to listen to Leo Buscaglia, because he speaks of such things as love, hugging, and being open to people.

(*e*) It is better not to listen to Leo Buscaglia, because though Leo's entertaining, both you and Leo are going to feel worse afterwards.

(*f*) It is better to read the book you are presently reading, though not much better, because it does not tell you how to get over shyness, anxiety, and such, but only raises them as subjects between writer and reader and renders the unformulable formulable, for a while perhaps even tolerable.

(*g*) It is better not to seek help from a psychotherapist but to accept your shyness, painful though it is, because it is better to be your shy self than the sort of person the psychotherapist may want you to become, i.e., like the psychotherapist.

(*h*) It is better to seek help from a psychotherapist if the psychotherapist knows what not many psychotherapists know, namely, that the shy person may know something the non-shy person does not know, that your self is indeed unformulable to yourself, that you are entitled to your shyness, that, indeed, varying degrees of idiocy are required not to be shy, that the very unformulability of your self is the only clue you have to the uniqueness of yourself, that otherwise one will become yet another Ralph among a thousand Ralphs, or worse still, become an imitation of the psychotherapist.

(CHECK ONE)

Thought Experiment: In which of the two following situations would you find yourself more shy?

(1) Addressing an audience of 500 of your fellow townsmen

(2) Journeying to the Valley of the Blind, described in H. G. Wells's story, and addressing 500 strange people who cannot see you

Explain your choice.

Thought Experiment (II): You are invited to a party. You have a choice of going as any one of these four people. Which would you choose?

(*a*) Mickey Rooney, who (let us say) is not shy (though who knows for sure?), who comes into a room like a tornado

(*b*) Johnny Carson, who is terrified, who sidles along the wall in dark glasses hoping no one will speak to him and then is miserable because no one speaks to him (*c*) Yourself, who is shy and don't think you should be, therefore you spend all your energy concealing your terrible malady and trying to figure out how to correct it

(*d*) Yourself, who is shy, but who knows you're entitled and that everyone else is likely to be in the same fix, and who therefore accepts it like a prisoner thrown into the drunk tank with ten other people all strange to each other—which is what in fact you all are—and so are free to gaze at the others with a mild curiosity and free to ask simple-minded questions and make simple-minded requests, such as: What are you doing here? or: I notice you seem a little uptight and are breathing shallow—come over here, I'll put my hand on your diaphragm, take a deep breath; or: Let me tell you something interesting that happened to me today—nothing; or: My head is killing me, would you mind massaging my neck? or: My name is Jon Johnson and I come from Wisconsin—that's a fact—and I'm wondering whether I made a mistake in leaving, so I'm having two quick drinks, can I fix you two? or: You're good-looking and since there is clearly nothing for us to talk about, would you care to step outside to my car and fool around?

(CHECK ONE)

(7) THE MISPLACED SELF: *How Two Selves Confronting Each Other can Miscalculate, Each Attributing a Putative and Spurious Reality to the Other and Trying to Match it, with the Consequence that Both Selves Become Non-selves*

A filmmaker reported the following experience with his film company, especially the actors, while on location in a small Midwestern town.

The townspeople showed a tremendous excitement about the presence of the film company in their midst. Not only did they make the town and even their homes available to the film crew, allowing their very lives to be disrupted, some town folk even expressed the strongest possible desire to be in the film, if only in the most insignificant roles. A quiet woman, the librarian, said that it would be the greatest event of her life.

The actors also enjoyed their stay in the town and the attention they were getting. Even though they, the actors, were not held in the highest regard by the filmmakers—producers, directors, cinematographers, etc.—were in fact often referred to by the latter as "pieces of meat," "talking faces," "hollow heads" among other uncomplimentary expressions—they, the actors, found themselves playing enjoyable roles in the town. What roles? They were playing the roles of the superb human beings the town folk believed them to be. Everyone in town remarked what nice people they were. So they became nice. They became nicer than saints. One famous actress in particular, noted for her childish and difficult ways, became a very model of friendliness and graciousness, astounding even the film crew and the town folk by her small acts of kindness, such as inquiring after the health of a stagehand's sick child, remembering the name of the A & P checkout lady.

Question (I): Which of the two, the actors or the townspeople, are the more real, that is, perceive themselves as more nearly what they are?

(*a*) The townspeople, because they have no illusions about themselves, their humdrum lives and workaday selves, whereas the actors not only live in a tinsel world but are themselves forever playing roles, are always "on" even when they walk into the town drugstore.

(*b*) The actors, particularly the actress who, by very reason of her finding herself in a real place among real people and removed from the fakery of Hollywood, is able for once in her life to become herself, her true best self.

(*c*) Neither town folk nor actors, because both are equally displaced, equally deprived of themselves, though in different ways. The town folk are deprived because, though they live in a "real" town, through an optical illusion they perceive the actors to be more splendidly real than they themselves and perceive the actors' lives to be both more glamorous and more of a piece (to judge from the films) than their own, which seem somewhat dim and tentative by comparison. Through a different sort of optical illusion, the actors are able for a while to take on the very reality imputed to them by the town folk, wear it like a costume and with the greatest of ease because they've been doing nothing else most of their lives. Thus, they cloak the nought and nakedness of their selves, which are perhaps no different in kind from anyone else's but perhaps more acutely felt.

Note that the felt "reality" of the actors in the town is as brief as any other performance. After six weeks on location, even the gracious actress said she "couldn't wait to get out of the boonies." For their part, too, the town folk might get sick and tired of the antics of, say, Mel Brooks.

Though both actors and town folk have reached for what they perceived to be a heightened reality, it, reality itself, has somehow fallen between them, like a dropped ball.

Question (II): Test your own index of misplacement.

(1) Imagine meeting Robert Redford under the most ordinary circumstances: you're a bank teller and he comes in to cash a check. He is very nice, almost preternaturally nice. You perceive that Redford's self has, perhaps by virtue of his film image, a higher or at least a different reality from your own.

(2) Imagine that you are a movie star finding yourself in a small town, you with all the well-known self-problems of movie stars—What if these people recognize me and hassle me, about autographs? What if they *don't* recognize me?—and all the anxiety caused by three failed films, dearth of good scripts, unsympathetic directors, producers, and moneymen. Now imagine you as such a movie star watching the locals at work and play; you envy the A & P manager perched in the manager's box keeping an eye on the checkout lines, watering the lawn of a late summer evening.

Which of the two would you rather be, the bank teller or the movie star?

(CHECK ONE)

Thought Experiment: Imagine you are walking down Madison Avenue behind Al Pacino, whom you have seen frequently in the movies but never in the flesh. He is shorter than you thought. His raincoat is thrown over his shoulder. Hands in pockets, he stops to look in the window of Abercrombie & Fitch. His face takes on a characteristic expression, jaws clenched, eyes dark and luminous, like young Corleone in *The Godfather.* The sight of Pacino in the flesh acting like Pacino on the screen gives you a peculiar pleasure. Then you become aware that though Pacino is looking at the articles in the window display, he is also checking his own reflection in the glass. This, too, gives you pleasure, though of a different sort. Explain the difference. (Hint: The esthetic pleasure of seeing an instance of a symbol, Pacino in the flesh at Abercrombie's, measure up and conform to the symbol itself, Pacino on the screen, and the different pleasure of seeing the instance, Pacino, rescued from the symbol and restored to human creatureliness, the self in all its vagary, individuality, and folly. The first case: Ah, there is Pacino acting just like Corleone! The second case: Ah, there is Pacino acting just like me!)

(8) THE PROMISCUOUS SELF: *Why is it that One's Self often not only does not Prefer Sex with one's Chosen Mate, Chosen for His or Her Attractiveness and Suitability, even when the Mate is a Person well known to one, knowing of one, loved by one, with a Life, Time, and Family in common, but rather prefers Sex with a New Person, even a Total Stranger, or even Vicariously through Pornography*

A recent survey in a large city reported that 95 percent of all video tapes purchased for home consumption were *Insatiable*, a pornographic film starring Marilyn Chambers.

Of all sexual encounters on soap opera, only 6 percent occur between husband and wife.

In some cities of the United States, which now has the highest divorce rate in the world, the incidence of divorce now approaches 60 percent of married couples.

A recent survey showed that the frequency of sexual intercourse in married couples declined 90 percent after three years of marriage.

"A female sexologist reported . . ." that a favorite fantasy of American women, second only to oral sex, was having sex with two strange men at once.

According to the president of the North American Swing Club Association, only 3 percent of married couples who are swingers get divorces, as compared with over 50 percent of non-swinging couples.

In large American cities, lunch-break liaisons between business men and women have become commonplace.

Sexual activity and pregnancy in teenagers have increased dramatically in the last twenty years, in both those who have received sex education in schools and those who have not. In some cities, more babies are born to single women than to married women.

A radio psychotherapist reported that nowadays many young people who disdain marriage, preferring "relationships" and "commitments," speak of entering into simultaneous relationships with a second or third person as a growth experience.

In San Francisco's Buena Vista Park, to the outrage of local middle-class residents, homosexuals cruise and upon encountering a sexual prospect, always a stranger, exchange a word or a sign and disappear into the bushes. In a series of interviews, Buena Vista homosexuals admitted to sexual encounters with an average of more than 500 strangers.

A survey by a popular magazine reported that the incidence of homosexuality in the United States had surpassed that of the Weimar Republic and is approaching that of England.

Question: Do Americans, as well as other Westerners, prefer sexual variety, both heterosexual and homosexual, because

(*a*) The sexual revolution has occurred, which is nothing else but the overthrow of the unnatural repressions and taboos of 1,900 years of Christianity and the exploration of the free and healthy practices of a sexually liberated society.

(*b*) Humans are biologically as promiscuous as chimpanzees. It is only the cultural constraints of society, probably imposed by the economic necessities of an agricultural society, which required a monogamous union and children as a reliable labor source.

(c) No, man is by nature monogamous, as ethnologists have demonstrated in most cultures. It is Western society which is disintegrating, to a degree remarkably similar to the decline of the Roman Empire in the fifth century, when similar practices were reported.

(d) No, Western man is promiscuous because promiscuous sexuality is the obverse or flip side of Christianity and is in fact specified by Christianity as its opposite. Thus, pornography is something new in the world, having no parallel in ancient, so-called pagan cultures. Accordingly, there is little if any difference between present-day promiscuity and that of, say, the Victorian era. The so-called sexual revolution is nothing but the legitimizing of the secret behavior of the Victorians and its extension to women.

(e) Western man is promiscuous because something unprecedented has happened. As a consequence of the scientific and technological revolution, there has occurred a displacement of the real as a consequence of which genital sexuality has come to be seen as the substratum of all human relationships, of friendship, love, and the rest. This displacement has come to pass as a consequence of a lay misperception of the physicist's quest for establishing a molecular or energic basis for all interactions and of what is perceived as Freud's identification of genital sexuality as the ground of all human relationships.

A letter to Dear Abby:

> I am a twenty-three-year-old liberated woman who has been on the pill for two years. It's getting pretty expensive and I think my boyfriend should share half the cost, but I don't know him well enough to discuss money with him.*

---

* Abigail Van Buren, *The Best of Dear Abby* (New York: Andrews and McMeel, 1981), p. 242.

(*f*) The Self since the time of Descartes has been stranded, split off from everything else in the Cosmos, a mind which professes to understand bodies and galaxies but is by the very act of understanding marooned in the Cosmos, with which it has no connection. It therefore needs to exercise every option in order to reassure itself that it is not a ghost but is rather a self among other selves. One such option is a sexual encounter. Another is war. The pleasure of a sexual encounter derives not only from physical gratification but also from the demonstration to oneself that, despite one's own ghostliness, one is, for the moment at least, a sexual being. Amazing! Indeed, the most amazing of all the creatures of the Cosmos: a ghost with an erection! Yet not really amazing, for only if the abstracted ghost has an erection can it, like Jove spying Europa on the beach, enter the human condition.

(*g*) It's not that complicated. It's simply that people nowadays have too much money and time to spend and don't know what to do with themselves and so will try anything out of boredom.

(*h*) Why go further than the orthodox Judaeo-Christian belief that monogamous marriage was ordained by God for man's happiness, that the devil goes about like a roaring lion seeking whom he may devour, and that as a consequence modern man has lost his way, has not the faintest notion who he is or what he is doing, and nothing short of catastrophe will bring him to his senses. At the height of a hurricane, husbands come to themselves and can even embrace their wives. During hurricane Camille, one Biloxi couple, taking refuge in a tree house, reported that, during the passage of the eye, they had intercourse for the first time in years.

(*i*) No, the explanation is biological. Man is undergoing a mutation in sexual behavior which will in the end, like the tooth of the saber-toothed tiger, render him extinct. Since most of the emerging varieties of sexual expression—homosexuality, anal and oral sex—do not reproduce the species and therefore have no survival value, the species will become extinct.

(*j*) None of the above. It has always been so. That is to say, the sexual behavior of humans has not changed. Therefore, there is nothing to explain.

(CHECK ONE OR MORE)

Thought Experiment

THE LAST DONAHUE SHOW

The Donahue Show is in progress on what appears at first to be an ordinary weekday morning.

The theme of this morning's show is Donahue's favorite, sex, the extraordinary variety of sexual behavior—"sexual preference," as Donahue would call it—in the country and the embattled attitudes toward it. Although Donahue has been accused of appealing to prurient interest, with a sharp eye cocked on the ratings, he defends himself by saying that he presents these controversial matters in "a mature and tasteful manner"—which he often does. It should also be noted in Donahue's defense that the high ratings of these sex-talk shows are nothing more nor less than an index of the public's intense interest in such matters.

The guests today are:

Bill, a homosexual and habitué of Buena Vista Park in San Francisco

Allen, a heterosexual businessman, married, and a connoisseur of the lunch-hour liaison

Penny, a pregnant fourteen-year-old

Dr. Joyce Friday, a well-known talk-show sex therapist, or in media jargon: a psych jockey

BILL'S STORY: Yes, I'm gay, and yes, I cruise Buena Vista. Yes, I've probably had over five hundred encounters with lovers, though I didn't keep count. So what? Whose business is it? I'm gainfully employed by a savings-and-loan company, am a trustworthy employee, and do an honest day's work. My recreation is Buena Vista Park and the strangers I meet there. I don't molest children, rape women, snatch purses. I contribute to United Way. Such encounters that I do have are by mutual consent and therefore nobody's business—except my steady live-in friend's. Naturally he's upset, but that's our problem.

DONAHUE (*striding up and down, mike in hand, boyishly inarticulate*): C'mon, Bill. What about the kids who might see you? You know what I mean. I mean— (*Opens his free hand to the audience, soliciting their understanding*)

BILL: Kids don't see me. Nobody sees me.

DONAHUE (*coming close, on the attack but good-naturedly, spoofing himself as prosecutor*): Say, Bill. I've always been curious. Is there some sort of signal? I mean, how do you and the other guy know—help me out—

BILL: Eye contact, or we show a bit of handkerchief here. (*Demonstrates*)

STUDIO AUDIENCE: (*Laughter*)

DONAHUE (*shrugging [Don't blame me, folks], pushes up nose-bridge of glasses, swings mike over to Dr. J.F. without looking at her*): How about it, Doc?

DR. J.F. (*in her not-mincing-words voice*): I think Bill's behavior is immature and depersonalizing. (*Applause from audience*) I think he ought to return to his steady live-in friend and work out a mature, creative relationship. You might be interested to know that studies have shown that stable gay couples are more creative than straights. (*Applause again, but more tentative*)

DONAHUE (*eyes slightly rolled back, swings mike to Bill*): How about it, Bill?

BILL: Yeah, right. But I still cruise Buena Vista.

DONAHUE (*pensive, head to one side, strides backward, forward, then over to Allen*): How about you, Allen?

ALLEN'S STORY: I'm a good person, I think. I work hard, am happily married, love my wife and family, also support United Way, served in the army. I drink very little, don't do drugs, have never been to a porn movie. My idea of R & R— maybe I got it in the army—is to meet an attractive woman. What a delight it is, to see a handsome mature woman, maybe in the secretarial pool, maybe in a bar, restaurant, anywhere, exchange eye contact, speak to her in a nice way, respect her as a person, invite her to join me for lunch (no sexual harassment in the office—I hate that!), have a drink, two drinks, enjoy a nice meal, talk about matters of common interest— then simply ask her—by now, both of you know whether you like each other. What a joy to go with her up in the elevator of the downtown Holiday Inn, both of you silent, relaxed, smiling, anticipating— The door of the room closes behind you. You look at her, take her hand. There's champagne already there. You stand at the window with her, touch glasses, talk—there's nothing vulgar. No closed-circuit TV. Do you know what we did last time? We turned on *La Bohème* on the FM. She loves Puccini.

DONAHUE: C'mon, Allen. What are ya handing me? What d'ya mean you're happily married? You mean *you're* happy.

ALLEN: No, no. Vera's happy, too.

AUDIENCE (*mostly women, groaning*): Nooooooo.

DONAHUE: Okay-okay, ladies, hold it a second. What do you mean, Vera's happy? I mean, how do you manage—help me out, I'm about to get in trouble—hold the letters, folks—

ALLEN: Well, actually, Vera has a low sex drive. We've always been quite inactive, even at the beginning—

AUDIENCE (*groans, jumbled protests*): Nooooo.

DONAHUE (*backing away, holding up placating free hand, backing around to Dr. J.F.*): It's all yours, Doc.

DR. J.F.: Studies have shown that open marriages can be growth experiences for both partners. However—(*groans from audience*)—*However*: it seems to me that Vera may be getting the short end here. I mean, I don't know Vera's side of it. But could I ask you this? Have you and Vera thought about reenergizing your sex life?

ALLEN: Well, ah—

DR. J.F.: Studies have shown, for example, that more stale marriages have been revived by oral sex than any other technique—

DONAHUE: Now, Doc—

DR. J.F.: Other studies have shown that mutual masturbation—

DONAHUE (*eyes rolled back*): We're running long folks, we'll be right back after this—don't go away. Oh boy. (*Lets mike slide to the hilt through his hand, closes eyes, as camera cuts away to a Maxithins commercial*)

DONAHUE: We're back. Thank the good Lord for good sponsors. (*Turns to Penny, a thin, inattentive, moping teenager, even possibly a pre-teen*): Penny?

PENNY (*chewing something*): Yeah?

DONAHUE (*solicitous, quite effectively tender*): What's with you, sweetheart?

PENNY: Well, I liked this boy a lot and he told me there was one way I could prove it—

DONAHUE: Wait a minute, Penny. Now this, your being here, is okay with your parents, right? I mean let's establish that.

PENNY: Oh, sure. They're right over there—you can ask them. (*Camera pans over audience, settling on a couple with mild, pleasant faces. It is evident that on the whole they are not displeased with being on TV*)

DONAHUE: Okay. So you mean you didn't know about taking precautions—

DR. J.F. (*breaking in*): Now, that's what I mean, Phil.

DONAHUE: What's that, Doc?

DR. J.F.: About the crying need for sex education in our schools. Now if this child—

PENNY: Oh, I had all that stuff at Ben Franklin.

DONAHUE: You mean you knew about the pill and the other, ah—

PENNY: I had been on the pill for a year.

DONAHUE (*scratching head*): I don't get it. Oh, you mean you slipped up, got careless?

PENNY: No, I did it on purpose.

DONAHUE: Did what on purpose? You mean—

PENNY: I mean I wanted to get pregnant.

DONAHUE: Why was that, Penny?

PENNY: My best friend was pregnant.

AUDIENCE: (*Groans, laughter*)

DR. J.F.: You see, Phil, that's just what I mean. This girl is no more equipped with parenting skills than a child. She is a child. I hope she realizes she still has viable options.

DONAHUE: How about it, Penny?

PENNY: No, I want to have my baby.

DONAHUE: Why?

PENNY: I think babies are neat.

DONAHUE: Oh boy.

DR. J.F.: Studies have shown that unwanted babies suffer 85 percent more child abuse and 150 percent more neuroses later in life.

DONAHUE (*striding*): Okay, now what have we got here? Wait. What's going on?

There is an interruption. Confusion at the rear of the studio. Heads turn. Three strangers, dressed outlandishly, stride down the aisle.

DONAHUE (*smacks his forehead*): What's this? What's this? Holy smoke!

Already the audience is smiling, reassured both by Donahue's comic consternation and by the exoticness of the visitors. Clearly, the audience thinks, they are part of the act.

The three strangers are indeed outlandish.

One is a tall, thin, bearded man dressed like a sixteenth-century reformer. Indeed, he could be John Calvin, in his black cloak, black cap with short bill, and snug earflaps.

The second wears the full-dress uniform of a Confederate officer. Though he is a colonel, he is quite young, surely no more than twenty-five. Clean-shaven and extremely handsome, he looks for all the world like Colonel John Pelham, Jeb Stuart's legendary artillerist. Renowned both for his gallantry in battle and for his chivalry toward women, the beau ideal of the South, he engaged in sixty artillery duels, won them all, lost not a single piece. With a single Napoleon, he held off three of Burnside's divisions in front of Fredericksburg before being ordered by Stuart to retreat.

The third is at once the most ordinary-looking and yet the strangest of all. His dress is both modern and out-of-date. In his light-colored double-breasted suit and bow tie, his two-tone shoes of the sort known in the 1940s as "perforated wing-tips," his neat above-the-ears haircut, he looks a bit like the clean old man in the Beatles movie *A Hard Day's Night*, a bit like Lowell Thomas or perhaps Harry Truman. It is as if he were a visitor from the Cosmos, from a planet ten or so light-years distant, who had formed his notion of earthlings from belated transmissions of 1950 TV, from watching the Ed Sullivan Show, old Chester Morris movies, and Morey Amsterdam. Or, to judge from his speaking voice, he could have been an inveterate listener during the Golden Age of radio and modeled his speech on that of Harry Von Zell.

DONAHUE (*backpedaling, smacking his head again*): Holy smoke! Who are these guys? (*Beseeching the audience with a slow comic pan around*)

The audience laughs, not believing for a moment that these latecomers are not one of Donahue's surprises. And yet—

DONAHUE (*snapping his fingers*): I got it. Wait'll I get that guy. It's Steve Allen, right? Refugees from the Steve Allen Show, *Great Conversations*? Famous historical figures? You know, folks, they do that show in the studio down the hall. Wait'll I get that guy.

General laughter. Everybody remembers it's been done before, an old show-biz trick, like Carson barging in on Rickles during the C.P.O. Sharkey taping.

DONAHUE: Okay already. Okay, who we got here? This is Moses? General Robert E. Lee? And who is this guy? Harry Truman? Okay, fellas, let's hear it. (*Donahue, an attractive fellow, is moving about as gracefully as a dancer*)

THE STRANGER (*speaks first, in his standard radio-announcer's voice, which is not as flat as the Chicagoans who say, Hyev a hyeppy New Year*): I don't know what these two are doing here, but I came to give you a message. We've been listening to this show.

DONAHUE (*winking at the audience*): And where were you listening to us?

STRANGER: In the green room.

DONAHUE: Where else? Okay. Then what do you think? Let's hear it first from the reverend here. What did you say your name was, Reverend?

STRANGER: John Calvin.

DONAHUE: Right. Who else? Okay, we got to break here for these messages. Don't go 'way, folks. We're coming right back and sort this out, I promise.

Cut to Miss Clairol, Land O Lakes margarine, Summer's Eve, and Alpo commercials.

But when the show returns, John Calvin, who does not understand commercial breaks, has jumped the gun and is in mid-sentence.

CALVIN (*speaking in a thick French accent, not unlike Charles Boyer*): —of his redemptive sacrifice? What I have heard is licentious talk about deeds which are an abomination before God, meriting eternal damnation unless they repent and throw themselves on God's mercy. Which they are pre-destined to do or not to do, so why bother to discuss it?

DONAHUE (*gravely*): That's pretty heavy, Reverend.

CALVIN: Heavy? Yes, it's heavy.

DONAHUE (*mulling, scratching*): Now wait a minute, Rev-erend. Let's check this out. You're entitled to your religious beliefs. But what if others disagree with you in all good faith? And aside from *that* (*prosecutory again, using mike like fore-finger*) what's wrong with two consenting adults expressing their sexual preference in the privacy of their bedroom or, ah, under a bush?

CALVIN: Sexual preference? (*Puzzled, he turns for help to the Confederate officer and the Cosmic stranger. They shrug*)

DONAHUE (*holding mike to the officer*): How about you, sir? Your name is—

CONFEDERATE OFFICER: Colonel John Pelham, C.S.A., commander of the horse artillery under General Stuart.

PENNY: He's cute.

AUDIENCE: (*Laughter*)

DONAHUE: You heard it all in the green room, Colonel. What 'dya think?

COLONEL PELHAM (*in a soft Alabama accent*): What do I think of what, sir?

DONAHUE: Of what you heard in the green room.

PELHAM: Of the way these folks act and talk? Well, I don't think much of it, sir.

DONAHUE: How do you mean, Colonel?

PELHAM: That's not the way people should talk or act. Where I come from, we'd call them white trash. That's no way to talk if you're a man or a woman. A gentleman knows how to treat women. He knows because he knows himself, who he is, what his obligations are. And he discharges them. But after all, you won the war, so if that's the way you want to act, that's your affair. At least, we can be sure of one thing.

DONAHUE: What's that, Colonel?

PELHAM: We're not sorry we fought.

DONAHUE: I see. Then you agree with the reverend, I mean Reverend Calvin here.

PELHAM: Well, I respect his religious beliefs. But I never thought much about religion one way or the other. In fact, I don't think religion has much to do with whether a man does right. A West Point man is an officer and a gentleman, religion or no religion. I have nothing against religion. In fact, when we studied medieval history at West Point, I remember admiring Richard Coeur de Lion and his recapturing Acre and the holy places. I remember thinking: I would have fought for him, just as I fought for Lee and the South.

Applause from the audience. Calvin puts them off, but this handsome officer reminds them of Rhett Butler–Clark Gable, or rather Ashley Wilkes–Leslie Howard.

DONAHUE (*drifting off, frowning; something is amiss but he can't put his finger on it. What is Steve Allen up to? He shakes his head, blinks*): You said it, Colonel. Okay. Where were we? (*Turning to Cosmic stranger*) We're running a little long. Can you make it brief, Harry—Mr. President, or whoever you are? Oh boy.

THE COSMIC STRANGER (*stands stiffly, hands at his sides, and begins speaking briskly, very much in the style of the late Raymond Gram Swing*): I will be brief. I have taken this human form through a holographic technique unknown to you in order to make myself understood to you.

Hear this. I have a message. Whether you heed it or not is your affair.

I have nothing to say to you about God or the Confederacy, whatever that is—I assume it is not the G2V Confederacy in this arm of the galaxy—though I could speak about God, but it is too late for you, and I am not here to do that.

We are not interested in the varieties of your sexual behavior, except as a symptom of a more important disorder.

It is this disorder which concerns us and which we do not fully understand.

As a consequence of this disorder, you are a potential threat to all civilizations in the G2V region of the galaxy. Throughout G2V you are known variously and jokingly as the Ds or the DDs or the DLs, that is, the ding-a-lings or the death-dealers or the death-lovers. Of all the species here and in all of G2V, you are the only one which is by nature sentimental, murderous, self-hating, and self-destructive.

You are two superpowers here. The other is hopeless, has already succumbed, and is a death society. It is a living death and an agent for the propagation of death.

You are scarcely better—there is a glimmer of hope for you—but that is of no interest to me.

If the two of you destroy each other, as appears likely, it is of no consequence to us. To tell you the truth, G2V will breathe a sigh of relief.

The danger is that you may not destroy each other and that your present crude technology may constitute a threat to G2V in the future.

I am here to tell you three things: what is going to happen, what I am going to do, and what you can do.

Here's what will happen. Within the next twenty-four hours, your last war will begin. There will occur a twenty-megaton airburst one mile above the University of Chicago, the very site where your first chain reaction was produced. Every American city and town will be hit. You will lose plus-minus 160 million immediately, plus-minus 50 million later.

Here's what I am going to do. I have been commissioned to collect a specimen of DD and return with it so that we can study it toward the end of determining the nature of your disorder. Accordingly, I propose to take this young person referred to as Penny—for two reasons. One, she is perhaps still young enough not to have become hopeless. Two, she is pregnant and so we will have a chance to rear a DD in an environment free of your noxious influence. Then perhaps we can determine whether your disorder is a result of some peculiar earth environmental factor or whether you are a malignant sport, a genetic accident, the consequence of what you would have called, quite accurately, in an earlier time an MD—*mutatio diabolica*, a diabolical mutation.

Finally, here's what you can do. It is of no consequence to

us whether you do it or not, because you will no longer be a threat to anyone. This is only a small gesture of goodwill to a remnant of you who may survive and who may have the chance to start all over—though you will probably repeat the same mistake. We have been students of your climatology for years. I have here a current read-out and prediction of the prevailing wind directions and fallout patterns for the next two weeks. It so happens that the place nearest you which will escape all effects of both blast and fallout is the community of Lost Cove, Tennessee. We do not anticipate a stampede to Tennessee. Our projection is that very few of you here and you out there in radio land will attach credibility to this message. But the few of you who do may wish to use this information. There is a cave there, corn, grits, collard greens, and smoked sausage in abundance.

That is the end of my message. Penny—

DONAHUE: We're long! We're long! Heavy! Steve, I'll get you for this. Oh boy. Don't forget, folks, tomorrow we got surrogate partners and a Kinsey panel—come back—you can't win 'em all—'bye! Grits. I dunno.

AUDIENCE: (*Applause*)

Cut to station break, Secure Card 65 commercial, Alpo, Carefree Panty Shields, and Mentholatum, then *The Price Is Right*.

Question: If you heard this Donahue Show, would you head for Lost Cove, Tennessee?

(*a*) Yes
(*b*) No

(CHECK ONE)

(9) THE ENVIOUS SELF *(in the root sense of envy: invidere, to look at with malice): Why it is that the Self—though it Professes to be Loving, Caring, to Prefer Peace to War, Concord to Discord, Life to Death; to Wish Other Selves Well, not Ill—in fact Secretly Relishes Wars and Rumors of War, News of Plane Crashes, Assassinations, Mass Murders, Obituaries, to say nothing of Local News about Acquaintances Dropping Dead in the Street, Gossip about Neighbors Getting in Fights or being Detected in Sexual Scandals, Embezzlements, and other Disgraces*

Everyone remembers where he was and what he was doing when he heard the news of the Kennedy assassination—or, if he is old enough, Pearl Harbor.

Why?

The self deceives itself by saying that it is natural that such terrible events should be etched in the memory.

It is not so simple.

The fact is that the scene and the circumstances of hearing such news become invested with a certain significance and density which they do not ordinarily possess and with which ordinary events and ordinary occasions contrast unfavorably.

Two such recollections as reported to me:

(1) I was standing outside a grocery store on the corner of St. Charles and Jackson Avenues in New Orleans when a stranger came up to me and said that the President had been shot and killed. I can remember noticing that the stranger wore an old-fashioned shirt, the kind with a tab collar and

a gold pin which fitted little holes in the tabs and kept the collar snug against the neck. Everything seemed amazingly vivid and discrete. I could even see the threads sewn in the little holes of the man's tab collar. Then he began to tell me the story of his life. He, too, felt curiously dispensed. I can even remember exactly where I stood on the sidewalk and a sycamore tree growing through a hole in the concrete. I can still see the bark.

Question: Had you noticed the tree before?

No.

Question: Have you noticed it since?

No.

(2) I was watching the soap opera *As the World Turns* on TV. It was a scene between Chris Hughes and Grandpa. A bulletin was flashed on the screen. *Bulletin: Shots have been fired into the Presidential motorcade in Dallas.* As the bulletin came on, Grandpa was saying to Chris Hughes something like: "Now let's don't be too hasty, Chris. I don't believe Ellen would do such a thing." I can remember thinking how unimportant the soap opera seemed compared with the events in Dallas.

Question: But before that, the soap opera seemed more interesting than the events in Dallas?

Yes.

Question: And since? Have you resumed watching *As the World Turns?*

Yes.

Question: During the week following Pearl Harbor, the incidence of suicide declined dramatically across the nation. Was this decline a consequence of

(1) A rise in patriotic fervor and a sense of purpose?

(2) A new sense of interest (e.g., something, even war, is better than nothing. Peace in the 1930s was like nothing)?

A Short Journal Chronicling Certain Events in Our Town

Monday. Everyone is cheerful today. Mr. D——, a well-known judge and gubernatorial candidate, was detected in an act of fellatio with a bellboy in the men's room of the Roosevelt Hotel during lunch hour. He was arrested by the vice squad. It is on the five o'clock news. Men stop each other in the street, shaking their heads: "Did you hear the awful thing that happened to Judge D——?" "Yes. I don't believe it. I think it's political. He was set up." "Right. Clearly, entrapment." Telephone lines are buzzing all over town. Housewives stop watching talk shows and soap operas to call each other.

Tuesday. Everyone in town is moderately depressed. Mr. L——, a highly successful attorney, a cheerful and generous man, wins the biggest lawsuit of his career, a ten-million-dollar judgment against A.T.&T. On the same day, he learns that his wife has been awarded the *Times-Picayune* cup for outstanding service to the community, his son has won a Rhodes Scholarship, and his daughter has been chosen to be Queen of the Comus Ball. His friends congratulate him. "You really hit the jackpot!" they exclaim and turn away with preoccupied expressions. The telephone wires do not hum. Housewives watch more soap operas than ever.

Wednesday. The ex-Premier of France, General de Gaulle, has died and the President of the United States attends his funeral. He looks very solemn and dignified sitting in Notre Dame cathedral. Later he confides to an aide that he enjoys state funerals more than anything he does in Washington or even Camp David because he can relax and let his mind go blank and yet be admired for paying his respects and taking so much trouble when all he has to do is look solemn. And also because there is de Gaulle dead as a duck and here I am alive and kicking.

Questions: Imagine yourself in a place most familiar to you and therefore most nugatory; e.g., standing on the platform of the commuter station at 8:00 a.m. on a Tuesday morning waiting for the 8:05 to New York. Or walking across your front yard in Montclair for the eight thousandth time to pick up the morning paper.

Now imagine that in these circumstances you receive a piece of news, either by way of a newspaper headline, by word of mouth from a neighbor, or perhaps by overhearing a radio bulletin from a black youth carrying a Sony CF–520.

In each instance of news, check the correct answer. Hint: Use as your guide your altered perception of your surroundings and any change in mood—e.g., whether, as a result of hearing the news, your front yard becomes visible for the first time since you moved in, or whether it becomes more nugatory than usual; whether your usual morning depression deepens or lifts.

There are four possible answers: (*a*) The news is unrelievedly bad. (*b*) The news is putatively bad, that is, news which by all criteria should be bad but in which you nevertheless take a certain comfort. (*c*) The news is unrelievedly good. (*d*) The news is putatively good, that is, news which by all criteria ought to be good but which you find secretly depressing.

(1) *News bulletin:* A UFO has landed in Nebraska and vaporized Omaha. This news is for you

(*a*) Unrelievedly bad: After all, there is nothing good about the loss of several hundred thousand people.

(*b*) Putatively bad but secretly not so bad: I don't know anybody in Omaha and there is something extremely interesting about an authenticated UFO visitation—which I had never really credited until now.

(CHECK ONE)

(2) While you stand at the paper-tube reading the morning headlines, a highly localized yet extremely violent tornado descends upon your house, carrying it aloft and away like Judy Garland's house in *The Wizard of Oz*. Your wife is in the house. Nothing is ever heard again of the house or your wife.

This event is

(*a*) Unrelievedly bad news: You love your wife. She is a good woman, your companion and helpmate for these twenty years. Your house, moreover, is underinsured.

(*b*) Putatively bad news: All the above is true enough, yet if the entire truth be known, your wife is also a shrew; you are sick to death of her, the house, your job, and your life. Since your wife has vanished through no fault of yours, cannot indeed have suffered much, whatever her fate, could indeed have been set down in a new place and a new life of her own like Judy, you are free to begin a new life without guilt.

(CHECK ONE)

(3) You are a woman whose husband has taken early retirement. He is a decent fellow, a combat veteran of Korea, and has been a good provider for thirty years. Money is no problem. Now, even though he is seriously overweight, all he does is sit around your pleasant Lake Wales house polishing off six-packs and watching golf, the NBA and NFL on TV. For months he goes without touching you and hardly speaking. Or he'll have spells of satyriasis when he'll want to have beery sex twice a night. What do you want? (What do women want?) You want to take a cathedral tour of Europe, or a leisurely barge voyage through the canals of France, stopping off at quaint French villages, or a cuisine tour through the vineyards and kitchens of the Loire Valley. Or visit the Galapagos Islands with your local Audubon Society.

He won't go. Why do I want to go look at a bunch of turtles? What does he want? He wants to go to Vegas to catch Wayne Newton and Liberace, or to Augusta to follow Nicklaus. You won't go. Yet you don't feel free to go off without him—you have duties as a housewife.

So one day you pick up a brochure from a travel agency in Orlando about a thatched-roof-cottage tour of England and a hot-air balloon ride down the Loire Valley and get in your car and start home. From the radio comes news of yet another sinkhole in the fragile limestone crust of central Florida. When you arrive in your block, you discover that your entire lot, house, husband Ralph, and the Zenith Chromacolor have dropped out of sight and disappeared forever into the Eocene muck.

This is

(*a*) Unrelievedly bad news: Ralph, a good man, a good husband, is gone. You, a good Christian woman, have lost your better half. You are alone in the world.

(*b*) Putatively bad: This is all true, but on the other hand Ralph is gone through no fault of your own and you are free. Frankly, thirty years of Ralph is enough. Moreover, Ralph was well insured.

(CHECK ONE)

(4) You are picking up the morning paper before going to work. It is a big day in your career. You are making a sales presentation to representatives of the biggest prospective corporate customer in the history of your firm. You've been suffering some anxiety and sleepless nights, and with good reason. In recent months you've been somewhat depressed and you're drinking more than you should.

A young insane person, totally unknown to you, drives slowly past your house in an ancient VW, takes aim with his

Colt Woodsman .22-caliber pistol, and shoots you in the arm-pit just as you reach to take the newspaper from the paper-tube.

The wound is probably not fatal. The bullet hits a rib, flattens, ricochets into the substance of your lung, but without injuring heart or major vessel. Your neighbor comes to your aid, calls an ambulance. Feeling faint, you sit on the grass of your front yard. You notice a dogwood tree which you planted ten years ago. It is doing well.

In the emergency room of the hospital, you feel a strange euphoria. You joke with the doctors. Even though you're spitting blood and growing fainter, your mind works wonderfully well. To the amazement of the doctors and nurses, you remember a remark of Churchill's, which you quote: "Nothing makes a man feel better than to be shot without effect."

Is this occurrence

(*a*) Unrelievedly bad news? It is not good to get shot. One could die of it.

(*b*) Putatively bad news but secretly good? The incident somehow dispenses you. The single irrational act of a madman changes the entire state of your life in an instant—from that of an anxious worried businessman in danger of losing a big account, to that of an innocent victim, not only not guilty but also unfailed, a patient who finds himself not only in the peculiar role of hospital patient with its peculiar prerogatives, that of being the passive and blameless recipient of the expert services of highly trained people, but of a certain honorific status as well, better than a business bonus: that of being a kind of surrogate victim for all of us. After all, it could happen to any of us in this crazy world, and here it has happened to you, a highly respected and successful member of the community. You took a round which any of us could have taken.

What is more, you'll probably get the account for your firm—which in your anxiety you might have lost—without lifting a finger. What corporation would turn you down?

Why did President Reagan feel better after he was shot than he has felt since?

(CHECK ONE)

(5) You are standing by your paper-tube in Englewood reading the headlines. Your neighbor comes out to get his paper. You look at him sympathetically. You know he has been having severe chest pains and is facing coronary bypass surgery. But he is not acting like a cardiac patient this morning. Over he jogs in his sweat pants, all smiles. He has triple good news. His chest ailment turned out to be a hiatal hernia, not serious. He's got a promotion and is moving to Greenwich, where he can keep his boat in the water rather than on a trailer.

"Great, Charlie! I'm really happy for you."

Are you happy for him?

(a) Yes. Unrelievedly good news. Surely it is good news all around that Charlie is alive and well and not dead or invalided. Surely, too, it is good for him and not bad for you if he also moves up in the world, buys a house in Greenwich where he can keep a 25-foot sloop moored in the Sound rather than a 12-foot Mayflower on a trailer in the garage in Englewood.

(b) Putatively good news but—but what? But the trouble is, it is good news for Charlie, but you don't feel so good.

(CHECK ONE)

If your answer is (b), could you specify your dissatisfaction, i.e., do the following thought experiment: which of the following news vis-à-vis Charlie and you at the paper-tube would make you feel better:

(1) Charlie is dead.

(2) Charlie has undergone a quadruple coronary bypass and may not make it.

(3) Charlie does not have heart trouble but he did not get his promotion or his house in Greenwich.

(4) Charlie does not have heart trouble and did get his promotion but can't afford to move to Greenwich.

(5) You, too, have received triple good news, so both of you can celebrate.

(6) You have not received good news, but just after hearing Charlie's triple good news, you catch sight of a garbage truck out of control and headed straight for Charlie—whose life you save by throwing a body block that knocks him behind a tree. (Why does it make you feel better to save Charlie's life and thus turn his triple good news into quadruple good fortune?)

(7) You have not received good news, but just after you hear Charlie's triple good news, an earthquake levels Manhattan. There the two of you stand, gazing bemused at the ruins across the Hudson from Englewood Cliffs.

(CHECK ONE)

In a word, how much good news about Charlie can you tolerate without compensatory catastrophes, heroic rescues, and such?

(6) On the station platform, a fellow commuter, a stranger to you these past six years, approaches you and tells you of the news bulletin he has just picked up from his Sony Mystereo. Not Manhattan but San Francisco has at last suffered the long-awaited major earthquake, magnitude 8.3 Richter. Casualties are estimated at near two hundred thousand.

(a) Unrelievedly bad news? How can there be anything good in such massive suffering and loss of life?

(*b*) Putatively bad news? Else why is your fellow commuter so excited that, even as he shakes his head dolefully, his earphones come loose? Does he take comfort in what he does not say but perhaps thinks, that it is Gomorrah getting its due, what with the gays, creeps, and deviates who must comprise at least half the casualties?

(CHECK ONE)

(7) You are an astronomer, starship designer, TV personality. You write about the Cosmos. You live next door to another astronomer, starship designer, TV personality. He also writes about the Cosmos. You both are employed by the Jet Propulsion Laboratory in Pasadena, not so much for your scientific abilities as for your PR value and your skill at popularizing science. You both have written best-sellers about space travel, ETIs (extraterrestrial intelligences), the necessity for nuclear disarmament, and so on. You are both aware that man might well destroy himself and the earth before he can explore the Cosmos and establish communication with other civilizations. There is a friendly rivalry between you. You two have different solutions to man's problems with himself.

You believe that wars are the consequences of sexually repressive societies, especially Christian. You have evidence that in more primitive societies, where sexual freedom is encouraged among both the young and adults, where there is an uninhibited display of affection and sexual contact, there are few if any wars. Your all-time favorite book is *Coming of Age in Samoa*. Your own latest book, *Space and Sexuality*, a best-seller, advances a proposal to create just such a society in miniature, a small community which is not only scientifically advanced but also loving and sexually unrepressed. Toward this end, you have designed a starship adapted from the Bussard fusion ramjet, which will accom modate a crew of ten (five men and five women), chosen not only for their technological skills but also for their freedom from sexual hang-ups, for a journey of several years to the vicinity of Alpha Centauri. The starship has already been jokingly nicknamed the Love Boat by your colleagues. But in all seriousness, you propose that NASA initiate a crash program to launch the ship before what you are almost certain will be the last war on earth.

You have been invited to appear tonight on the Tom Snyder Show to promote your new book, *Space and Sexuality*.

Your neighbor and friend has also written a book and has been invited to appear on the Johnny Carson Show—which has a higher rating in the sweeps than Snyder. To tell the truth, his book sales exceed yours. You two do not disagree in your understanding of the Cosmos and in your assessment of man's danger to himself. Yet your solutions are different. He believes that world peace can be achieved only by uniting the Western tradition of science and technology and the Eastern tradition of self-transcendence, especially Zen and Tibetan Buddhism.

In his book, *Space and Satori*, a version of the British starship Daedalus, powered by nuclear fusion, is proposed, the crew to be commanded by an experienced astronaut but with a spiritual leader on board, the noted Tibetan mystic Ti Chen.

Tonight, your neighbor, Dr. L——, and Ti will promote their book, *Space and Satori*, on the Carson Show. Both of you know that it is more desirable to be on the Carson Show than on the Tom Snyder Show.

As you make your morning trip to the paper-tube, you meet not Dr. L—— but his wife, who has bad news. She has reached her paper-tube first and is holding aloft the *L.A. Times*. There on the front page is an article exposing a sexual scandal at the Ti Chen Institute at La Jolla. Described by a disaffected disciple as an orgy, an incident is described in which Ti Chen is alleged to have engaged in a debauch with some of his young male disciples, in the course of which your neighbor, Dr. L——, appeared unexpectedly, flew into a jealous rage, and assaulted Ti Chen with a broken bottle. Everyone at the institute, in various states of undress, was arrested by the La Jolla police.

"Can you believe such crap!" cries your neighbor's wife, in a tearful rage, and slaps the *L.A. Times*. "I mean, my God, this you would expect from the *National Enquirer*. The same tissue of lies. I'm going to sue the bastards. Wouldn't you?"

You nod gravely and solicitously. This is bad news, indeed. This could mean the end of Dr. L——'s career at NASA, the end of his "scientific Buddhism." His wife says: "Would you believe Carson canceled him tonight?"

You shake your head, one arm around Dr. L——'s wife, patting her solicitously.

You grow thoughtful. Taken altogether, this is

(*a*) Unrelievedly bad news.
(*b*) Putatively bad news.

(CHECK ONE)

(8) You are one of two distinguished Southern writers in residence at Yaddo and living in neighboring cottages. You are both men of letters, noted for your poetry, fiction, and criticism. For years, even though you both live in Massachusetts, you have both attacked the crass, materialistic, money-grubbing society of the North and defended the traditional, agrarian, Christian values of the South, with its strong sense of place, family, and roots.

After a day of work, Writer *A* meets Writer *B*, as is their wont, on a pleasant woodland path to the dining room. The excited hostess of Yaddo breaks the rule of silence and accosts them in the woods. She has news that won't keep. Dan Rather has just announced it on the six o'clock news: Writer *B* has just won the Nobel Prize for literature!

Writer *A* embraces Writer *B* warmly. *B* shrugs: We both know what we think of the Nobel, etc. Yet *B* looks pleased. Whatever they think of the Nobel—e.g., people like John Steinbeck and Pearl Buck getting it, Joyce not getting it—it comes to over $200,000. Writer *B* looks pleased. Writer *A* horses around a bit, dares *B* to do a Sartre and turn it down, but still and all shows his pleasure: I'm so damned pleased for you.

If you are *A*, are you

(*a*) Unrelievedly pleased.

(*b*) Putatively pleased.

(CHECK ONE)

(10) THE BORED SELF: *Why the Self is the only Object in the Cosmos which Gets Bored*

The word *boredom* did not enter the language until the eighteenth century. No one knows its etymology. One guess is that *bore* may derive from the French verb *bourrer*, to stuff.

Question: Why was there no such word before the eighteenth century?

(*a*) Was it because people were not bored before the eighteenth century? (But wasn't Caligula bored?)

(*b*) Was it because people were bored but didn't have a word for it?

(*c*) Was it because people were too busy trying to stay alive to get bored? (But what about the idle English royalty and noblemen?)

(*d*) Is it because there is a special sense in which for the past two or three hundred years the self has perceived itself as a leftover which cannot be accounted for by its own objective view of the world and that in spite of an ever heightened self-consciousness, increased leisure, ever more access to cultural and recreational facilities, ever more instruction on self-help, self-growth, self-enrichment, the self feels ever more imprisoned in itself—no, worse than imprisoned because a prisoner at least knows he is imprisoned and sets store by the freedom awaiting him and the world to be open, when in fact the self is not and it is not—a state of affairs which has to be called something besides imprisonment—e.g., boredom. Boredom is the self being stuffed with itself.

(*e*) Is it because of a loss of sovereignty in which the self yields up plenary claims to every sector of the world to the respective experts and claimants of these sectors, and that such a surrender leads to an impoverishment which must be called by some other name, e.g., boredom?

(*f*) Is it because the self first had the means of understanding itself through myth, albeit incorrectly, later understood itself through religion as a creature of God, and now has the means of understanding the Cosmos through positive science but not itself because the self cannot be grasped by positive science, and that therefore the self can perceive itself only as a ghost in a machine? How else can a ghost feel otherwise toward a machine than bored?

(CHECK ONE OR MORE)

Question: Why is it no other species but man gets bored? Under the circumstances in which a man gets bored, a dog goes to sleep.

Thought Experiment: Imagine that you are a member of a tour visiting Greece. The group goes to the Parthenon. It is a bore. Few people even bother to look—it looked better in the brochure. So people take half a look, mostly take pictures, remark on the serious erosion by acid rain. You are puzzled. Why should one of the glories and fonts of Western civilization, viewed under pleasant conditions—good weather, good hotel room, good food, good guide—be a bore?

Now imagine under what set of circumstances a viewing of the Parthenon would not be a bore. For example, you are a NATO colonel defending Greece against a Soviet assault. You are in a bunker in downtown Athens, binoculars propped on sandbags. It is dawn. A medium-range missile attack is under way. Half a million Greeks are dead. Two missiles bracket the Parthenon. The next will surely be a hit. Between columns of smoke, a ray of golden light catches the portico.

Are you bored? Can you see the Parthenon?

Explain.

(11) THE DEPRESSED SELF: *Whether the Self is Depressed because there is Something Wrong with it or whether Depression is a Normal Response to a Deranged World*

The suicide rate among persons under twenty-five has risen dramatically in the last twenty years.

A recent survey disclosed that the symptom of depression outnumbered all other medical symptoms put together.

On a daytime radio psychotherapy talk show, 80 percent of all women calling in reported that they were depressed.

The incidence of drug use in teenagers and pre-teens has increased an estimated 3000 percent in the last thirty years. On a recent talk show on "tough love," it was claimed that about one-third of all teenagers were depressed. Of the one-third, as many as 75 percent were on drugs.

In one small Southern city, a study of the families of the upper socioeconomic class revealed that 79 percent of the daughters left home after high school, moved into apartments, and either attended college or got jobs. After five years, 53 percent of the unmarried daughters had returned to the homes of their parents and 43 percent of the married daughters . . . Typical responses: "I didn't like it out there." "It is too much." "I couldn't cope." "I got sad."

In one Midwestern town, 27 percent of high-school students dropped out and stayed home. Chief complaint: "I can't cope."

Question (I): Are people depressed despite unprecedented opportunities for education, vocations, self-growth, cultural enrichment, travel, and recreation

(*a*) Because modern life is more difficult, complex, and stressful than it has ever been before?

(*b*) Because, for men, competition in the marketplace is fiercer than ever?

(*c*) Because, for women, life as a housewife is lonelier than ever, what with the vanishing of the traditional community of women around the well, sitting on stoops, gossiping over back fences?

(*d*) Because, for young people, education is more inferior than ever, leaving one unprepared to face the real world?

(*e*) Because belief in God and religion has declined and with it man's confidence in the place of the self in the Cosmos, in the Chain of Being, and in its relation to others?

(*f*) Because the self nowadays is other-directed rather than inner-directed and depends for its self-esteem on its perception of how others evaluate it—something like a beggar in a crowd with his hand out?

(*g*) Because the self, despite an embarrassment of riches, is in fact impoverished and deprived, like Lazarus at the feast, having suffered a radical deprivation and loss of sovereignty? With the multiplication of technologies and the ascendence of experts and expertise in all fields, the self has consented to the expropriation of every sector of life by its appropriate expert—even the expropriation of its, the self's, own life. "I'm depressed, Doctor. What's wrong with me? If you are not an expert in the field, a doctor of depression, can you refer me to one?"

Thus, the rightful legatee of the greatest of fortunes, the cultural heritage of the entire Western World, its art, science, technology, literature, philosophy, religion, becomes a second-class consumer of these wares and as such disenfranchises itself and sits in the ashes like Cinderella yielding up ownership of its own dwelling to the true princes of the age, the experts. *They* know about science, *they* know about medicine, *they* know about government, *they* know about my needs, *they* know about everything in the Cosmos, even me. *They* know why I am fat and they know secrets of my soul which not even I know. There is an expert for everything that ails me, a doctor of my depression, a seer of my sadness.

(*b*) Because modern life is enough to depress anybody? Any person, man, woman, or child, who is not depressed by the nuclear arms race, by the modern city, by family life in the exurb, suburb, apartment, villa, and later in a retirement home, is himself deranged.

(CHECK ONE OR MORE)

Question (II): Why do so many teenagers, and younger people, turn to drugs?

(*a*) Because of peer-group pressure, failure of communication, psychological dysfunction, rebellion against parents, and decline of religious values.

(*b*) Because life is difficult, boring, disappointing, and unhappy, and drugs make you feel good.

(CHECK ONE)

Thought Experiment: A new cure for depression:

The only cure for depression is suicide.

This is not meant as a bad joke but as the serious proposal of suicide as a valid option. Unless the option is entertained seriously, its therapeutic value is lost. No threat is credible unless the threatener means it.

This treatment of depression requires a reversal of the

usual therapeutic rationale. The therapeutic rationale, which has never been questioned, is that depression is a symptom. A symptom implies an illness; there is something wrong with you. An illness should be treated.

Suppose you are depressed. You may be mildly or seriously depressed, clinically depressed, or suicidal. What do you usually do? Or what does one do with you? Do nothing or something. If something, what is done is always based on the premise that something is wrong with you and therefore it should be remedied. You are treated. You apply to friend, counselor, physician, minister, group. You take a trip, take anti-depressant drugs, change jobs, change wife or husband or "sexual partner."

Now, call into question the unspoken assumption: something is wrong with you. Like Copernicus and Einstein, turn the universe upside down and begin with a new assumption.

Assume that you are quite right. You are depressed because you have every reason to be depressed. No member of the other two million species which inhabit the earth—and who are luckily exempt from depression—would fail to be depressed if it lived the life you lead. You live in a deranged age—more deranged than usual, because despite great scientific and technological advances, man has not the faintest idea of who he is or what he is doing.

Begin with the reverse hypothesis, like Copernicus and Einstein. You are depressed because you should be. You are entitled to your depression. In fact, you'd be deranged if you were not depressed. Consider the only adults who are never depressed: chuckleheads, California surfers, and fundamentalist Christians who believe they have had a personal encounter with Jesus and are saved for once and all. Would you trade your depression to become any of these?

Now consider, not the usual therapeutic approach, but a

more ancient and honorable alternative, the Roman option. I do not care for life in this deranged world, it is not an honorable way to live; therefore, like Cato, I take my leave. Or, as Ivan said to God in *The Brothers Karamazov:* If you exist, I respectfully return my ticket.

Now notice that as soon as suicide is taken as a serious alternative, a curious thing happens. *To be or not to be* becomes a true choice, where before you were stuck with *to be.* Your only choice was how *to be* least painfully, either by counseling, narcotizing, boozing, groupizing, womanizing, man-hopping, or changing your sexual preference.

If you are serious about the choice, certain consequences follow. Consider the alternatives. Suppose you elect suicide. Very well. You exit. Then what? What happens after you exit? Nothing much. Very little, indeed. After a ripple or two, the water closes over your head as if you had never existed. You are not indispensable, after all. You are not even a black hole in the Cosmos. All that stress and anxiety was for nothing. Your fellow townsmen will have something to talk about for a few days. Your neighbors will profess shock and enjoy it. One or two might miss you, perhaps your family, who will also resent the disgrace. Your creditors will resent the inconvenience. Your lawyers will be pleased. Your psychiatrist will be displeased. The priest or minister or rabbi will say a few words over you and down you will go on the green tapes and that's the end of you. In a surprisingly short time, everyone is back in the rut of his own self as if you had never existed.

Now, in the light of this alternative, consider the other alternative. You can elect suicide, but you decide not to. What happens? All at once, you are dispensed. Why not live, instead of dying? You are free to do so. You are like a prisoner released from the cell of his life. You notice that the door to the cell is ajar and that the sun is shining outside. Why not take a walk down the street? Where you might have been dead, you are alive. The sun is shining.

Suddenly you feel like a castaway on an island. You can't believe your good fortune. You feel for broken bones. You are in one piece, sole survivor of a foundered ship whose captain and crew had worried themselves into a fatal funk. And here you are, cast up on a beach and taken in by islanders who, it turns out, are themselves worried sick—over what? Over status, saving face, self-esteem, national rivalries, boredom, anxiety, depression from which they seek relief mainly in wars and the natural catastrophes which regularly overtake their neighbors.

And you, an ex-suicide, lying on the beach? In what way have you been freed by the serious entertainment of your hypothetical suicide? Are you not free for the first time in your life to consider the folly of man, the most absurd of all the species, and to contemplate the comic mystery of your own existence? And even to consider which is the more absurd state of affairs, the manifest absurdity of your predicament: lost in the Cosmos and no news of how you got into such a fix or how to get out—or the even more preposterous eventuality that news did come from the God of the Cosmos, who took pity on your ridiculous plight and entered the space and time of your insignificant planet to tell you something.

The consequences of entertainable suicide? Lying on the beach, you are free for the first time in your life to pick up a coquina and look at it. You are even free to go home and, like the man from Chicago, dance with your wife.

The difference between a non-suicide and an ex-suicide leaving the house for work, at eight o'clock on an ordinary morning:

The non-suicide is a little traveling suck of care, sucking care with him from the past and being sucked toward care in the future. His breath is high in his chest.

The ex-suicide opens his front door, sits down on the steps, and laughs. Since he has the option of being dead, he has nothing to lose by being alive. It is good to be alive. He goes to work because he doesn't have to.

Mother Teresa of Calcutta recently remarked about some affluent Westerners she had met—including Americans, Europeans, capitalists, Marxists—that they seemed to her sad and poor, poorer even than the Calcutta poor, the poorest of the poor, to whom she ministered.

Question: What kind of impoverishment can be attributed to the denizens of Western technological societies in view of the obvious wealth of such societies in such categories as food, shelter, goods and services, education, technology, and cultural institutions?

(*a*) There is no such sadness and impoverishment. Mother Teresa makes such a charge because Western societies, with their increasing acceptance of contraceptive birth control and abortion, offend her Roman Catholic religious beliefs.

(*b*) There is, in fact, such a sadness and an impoverishment, due at least in part to a loss of respect for human life as evidenced not only by the acceptance of abortion but by mounting child abuse, euthanasia, and indifference to human suffering. Recent studies have shown, however, that Westerners, that is, Europeans and Americans, own more pets than ever and spend more money on pet food and veterinarians than the food costs of the entire Third World.

(*c*) There is such a sadness and impoverishment because in an affluent society, where there is a surfeit of goods and services, there is a corresponding devaluation. Whereas the poor peoples of the Third World, despite or because of their material deprivation, appreciate the simple things in life. Small is beautiful, the best things in life are free, etc.

(*d*) Because the poor in heart are blessed, i.e., receptive to the Gospel, whereas the rich may gain the whole world but lose their souls.

(*e*) Because Western society is an ethic of power and manipulation and self-aggrandizement at the expense of the values of community, love, innocence, simplicity, values encountered both in childhood and in non-aggressive societies (e.g., the Eskimo). As Ashley Montagu says, adulthood in the Western world is a deteriorated and impoverished childhood.

(*f*) Because Western society is itself a wasteland, its values decayed, its community fragmented, its morals corrupted, its cities in ruins. In the face of the deracination of Western culture, all talk of self-enrichment through this or that psychological technique is cosmetic, like rearranging the deck chairs of the *Titanic*. The Moral Majority is right. The only thing that can save us is a return to old-time religion, a revival of Christian Fundamentalism.

(*g*) None of the above. All arguments between the traditional scientific view of man as organism, a locus of needs and drives, and a Christian view of man as a spiritual being not only are unresolvable at the present level of discourse but are also profoundly boring—no small contributor indeed to the dreariness of Western society in general. The so-called détentes and reconciliations between "Science" and "Religion" are even more boring. What is more boring than hearing Heisenberg's uncertainty relations enlisted in support of the freedom of the will? The traditional scientific model of man is clearly inadequate, for a man can go to heroic lengths to identify and satisfy his needs and end by being more miserable than a Calcuttan. As for the present religious view of man, it begs its own question, the question of God's existence, which means that it is not only useless to the unbeliever but dispiriting. The latter is more depressed than ever at hearing the good news of Christianity. From the scientific view at least, a new model of man is needed, something other than man conceived as a locus of bio-psycho-sociological needs and drives.

Such an anthropological model might be provided by semiotics, that is, the study of man as the sign-using creature and, specifically, the study of the self and consciousness as derivatives of the sign-function.

Thought Experiment: If Mother Teresa is right and there exists in modern technological societies a paradoxical impoverishment in the midst of plenty, in the face of what is by traditional objective scientific criteria the most extensive effort in all of history to identify and satisfy man's biological, psychological, sociological, and cultural needs, consider a different model. Consider a more radical model than the conventional psycho-biological model, a semiotic model which allows one to explore the self in its nature and origins and to discover criteria for its impoverishment and wealth.

The following section, an intermezzo of some forty pages, can be skipped without fatal consequences. It is not technical but it is theoretical—i.e., it attempts an elementary semiotical grounding of the theory of self taken for granted in these pages. As such, it will be unsatisfactory to many readers. It will irritate many lay readers by appearing to be too technical—what does he care about semiotics? It will irritate many professional semioticists by not being technical enough —and for focusing on one dimension of semiotics which semioticists, for whatever reason, are not accustomed to regard as a proper subject of inquiry, i.e., not texts and other coded sign utterances but the self which produces texts or hears sign utterances.

A Semiotic* Primer of the Self

A Short History of the Cosmos with Emphasis on the Nature and Origin of the Self, plus a Semiotic Model for Computing Impoverishment in the Midst of Plenty, or Why it is Possible to Feel Bad in a Good Environment and Good in a Bad Environment

From the beginning and for most of the fifteen billion years of the life of the Cosmos, there was only one kind of event. It was particles hitting particles, chemical reactions, energy exchanges, gravity attractions between masses, field forces,

---

* Semiotics might be defined broadly as the science which deals with signs and the use of them by creatures. Here it will be read more narrowly as the human use of signs. Other writers include animal communication by signals, a discipline which Sebeok calls zoo-semiotics. But even the narrow use may be too broad. There is this perennial danger which besets semiotics: what with man being preeminently the sign-using creature, and what with man using signs in everything that he does, semiotics runs the risk of being about everything and hence about nothing.

At best a loose and inchoate discipline, semiotics is presently in such disarray that all sorts of people call themselves semioticists and come at the subject from six different directions. Accordingly, it seems advisable to define one's terms—there is not even agreement about what the word *sign* means—and to identify one's friends and foes.

The friends in this case, or at least the writers to whom I am most indebted, are: Ernst Cassirer, for his vast study of the manifold ways in which man uses the symbol, in language, myth, and art, as his primary means of articulating reality; Charles S. Peirce, founder of the modern discipline of semiotics and the first to distinguish clearly between the "dyadic" behavior of stimulus-response sequences and the "triadic" character of symbol-use; Ferdinand de Saussure, another founding father of semiotics, for his fruitful analysis of the human sign as the union of the signifier (*signifiant*) and the signified (*signifié*); Hans Werner, who systematically explored the process in which the signified is articulated within the form of the signifier; Susanne K. Langer, who, from the posture of behavioral science, clearly set forth the qualitative difference between animals' use of signals and man's use of symbols.

and so on. As different as such events are, they can all be understood as an interaction between two or more entities: A⇌B. Even a system as inconceivably vast as the Cosmos itself can be understood as such an interaction:

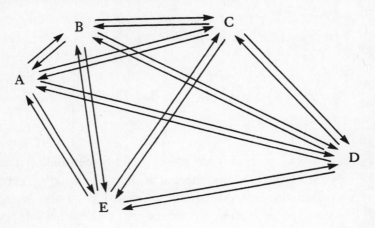

DIAGRAM 1

I am grateful for the important distinction, clearer in the German language and perhaps for this reason first arrived at by German thinkers, between *Welt* and *Umwelt*, or, roughly, world and environment, e.g., von Uexküll's *Umwelt* as, roughly, the significant environment within which an organism lives, and Heidegger's *Welt*, the "world" into which the *Dasein* or self finds itself "thrown"; also, Eccles' "World 3," the public domain of signs and language within which man—uniquely, according to Eccles—lives.

The foes? If there are foes, it is not because they have not made valuable contributions in their own disciplines, but because in this particular context, that of a semiotic of the self, they are either of no use or else hostile by their own declaration.

The first is the honorable tradition of American behaviorism, once so influential, and latter-day behaviorist semioticists like Charles Morris—honorable because of their rigorous attempt as good scientists to deal only with observables and so to bypass the ancient pitfalls of mind, soul, consciousness, and self which have bogged down psychologists for centuries. I start from the same place, looking at signs and the creatures which use them. My difficulty with the behaviorists is that they rule out mind, self, and consciousness as inaccessible either on the doctrinal grounds that they do not exist or on methodological grounds that they are beyond the reach of behavioral science.

It is not necessarily so. The value of Charles Peirce and social psycholo-

Every element in the Cosmos is in interaction with every other element. The elements and systems of the Cosmos are still in interaction whether we are speaking of the radiation of energy in the electromagnetic spectrum or the attraction of gravity between bodies. In a sense, astrologers are right. The planet Saturn has an influence on me; it exerts a small gravitational attraction. I in turn exert a slight pull not only on the planet Saturn but upon the entire M31 galaxy in Andromeda. When I take a single step, I affect the rotation of the earth.

---

gists like George Mead is that they underwrite the reality of the self without getting trapped in the isolated autonomous consciousness of Descartes and Chomsky. They do this by showing that the self becomes itself only through a transaction of signs with other selves—and does so, moreover, without succumbing to the mindless mechanism of the behaviorists.

The other semiotic foe is French structuralism—some of its proponents, at least—and its whimsical stepchild "deconstruction." The structuralists, in high fashion—at least until recently—seek to apply the methods of structural linguistics to such diverse matters as literature, myth, fashion, even cooking. Whatever the virtues of structuralism as a method of linguistics, ethnology, and criticism, it is the self-proclaimed foe, on what seem to be ideological grounds, of the very concept of the human subject. Lévi-Strauss boasts of the dehumanization which his structuralism implies. Michel Foucault argues that with the coming of semiotics the concept of the self has vanished from our new view of reality.

But this may not be the case.

I do not feel obliged to speak of the deconstructionists.

Finally, a terminological confusion needs to be straightened out. There is an almost intractable confusion about the terms *sign* and *symbol*. We may know what we mean when we say there is a difference between my dog's understanding of the word *ball*—to go and look for it—and your understanding of the same utterance—you may say "Ball? What about it?" —but we need to agree on what words to use to express the difference. Some writers (e.g., Peirce and Langer) would call the former *ball* a sign and the latter *ball* a symbol. Others would call the former a signal, the latter a sign. Though I have followed Peirce's usage in earlier writings, I propose here to use the word *signal* for the former and, following Saussure, the word *sign* for the latter, and to avoid *symbol* as much as possible. This usage seems advisable for two reasons. One is that *symbol* for most people seems to connote something emblematic like the flag or the cross and not the radical sense in which the common nouns of language are understood as symbols by Peirce, Cassirer, and Langer. The other reason is that the latter usage will be easier to reconcile with Saussure's valuable dissection of the sign into its two elements, signifier (*signifiant*) and signified (*signifié*).

II

Some three and a half billion years ago, organic life began on this planet, perhaps earlier on other planets, perhaps not at all. A discharge of lightning might have caused the formation of organic molecules in the primordial soup, molecules which sooner or later happened to replicate themselves, though it is difficult to imagine how these events could have occurred accidentally. Perhaps there was another cause. Perhaps God was the cause. We do not know. At any rate, a new kind of system came into being, the organism. It had the extraordinary property of maintaining its internal milieu, its homeostasis, and of reproducing itself. Yet, different though it was from other systems, events within the organism and across the membrane of the organism as well as events in its environment could still be understood as the same kind of events—dyadic interactions which had occurred before:

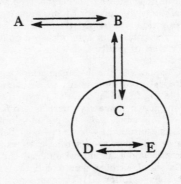

DIAGRAM 2

The interactions of organisms with each other, whether sexual, combative, or predatory, could be similarly understood:

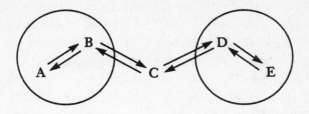

D I A G R A M 3

It is all very well to speak of the wonders of the Cosmos as testimony to the glory of God, and it may in fact be true, but it, the Cosmos, is hardly perceived as such in modern technological societies. For most scientists, it seems fair to say, these same wonders, including the behavior of organisms, can be explained as an interaction of elements. The wonder to the scientist is not that God made the world but that the works of God can be understood in terms of a mechanism without giving God a second thought. Is it not indeed more wonderful to understand the complex mechanisms (dyads) by which the DNA of a sperm joins with the DNA of an ovum to form a new organism than to have God snap his fingers and create an organism like a rabbit under a hat?

The real wonder is not that the Cosmos is now seen as wonderful but that it is not. Despite its inconceivable vastness, it is seen not as wonderful but as something that can be explained as a dyadic system.

III

It became useful to think of an organism as an open system which through the selective processes of evolution had developed a genetic code which enabled it to maintain an internal steady state (homeostasis) in a changing environment and to reproduce itself. Thus, all the elements and events in the Cosmos, including other organisms, could be thought of as the *environment* of the organism. The organism "responded" to those segments of its environment to which, through evolution, it had become genetically coded —hard-wired—to respond: eating, fighting, avoiding some, approaching and mating with others. Those segments of the environment which were without biological significance were ignored:

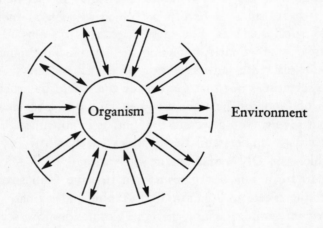

DIAGRAM 4

There are many gaps in the environment of an organism. This is to say that though there may be an interaction between the mass of the organism and the mass of Jupiter, the organism does not respond to Jupiter in any observable way. Yet the organism, as in the case of a migrating bird, has been shown to respond to the magnetic field of the earth or the position of the sun.

IV

An organism may also, either by being genetically coded or by learning—that is, by modifying certain neurones in its central nervous system—respond to certain signals in its environment by a behavior oriented toward other segments of the environment. Thus, a Texas leaf-cutting ant which discovers a food source too big to move will deposit a trail of pheromones on the ground, which other ants will follow for several hundred meters from the nest:

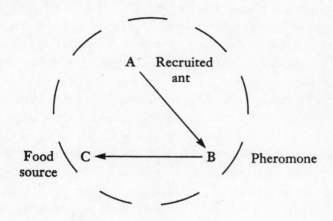

DIAGRAM 5

The Texas leaf-cutting ant is genetically programmed so to respond. But Pavlov's dog—or any other mammal exposed to certain changes in its environment—can *learn* to respond to a signal in an appropriate manner—by eating, fleeing, or fighting—through modification of cells in its central nervous system.

A gorilla (*A*) in its natural state can utter one of a dozen or so vocal signals which are responded to by other gorillas

(B, C, . . .) in an appropriate fashion—e.g., the bark *wraagh* is a signal of a sudden alarming situation, such as unexpected contact with buffalo, which signals flight in other gorillas.

The chimpanzee Lana has been taught by the Rumbaughs, through a learning program of rewards, to punch the differently marked keys of a computer and "ask" for food, liquids, music, etc.

Next the Rumbaughs taught two chimpanzees to communicate with each other, e.g., one chimp punching a marked key to ask another chimp for a certain food to which the importuned chimp had access. The Rumbaughs called the marks on the computer keys "symbols" and the transaction between the two chimps "the first successful demonstration of symbolic communication between two nonhuman primates."

Whereupon B. F. Skinner showed that two domestic pigeons (*Columba livia domestica*) could learn spontaneously to use such "symbols" to communicate with each other. The two pigeons, named Jack and Jill, could conduct a "conversation." Jack was the observer and Jill the informer. Jack and Jill first learned to associate marked keys with three colors. Jill was taught to "name" three colors in response to the keyboard-question "What color?" Jack was taught to select the color corresponding to the name. When the pigeons were correct, they were rewarded with grain. Then Jack learned to ask Jill for a color name by depressing the WHAT COLOR? key. Then Jill looked behind a curtain at a color hidden from Jack. Then, while Jack watched, Jill selected a "symbolic name" for the color. When Jill was right, Jack rewarded her by pushing the THANK YOU key. Then, while Jill moved to her reward, Jack selected the right color. Then Jack was rewarded.

Whether Skinner was out to discomfit the Rumbaughs and prove that pigeons are as smart as chimps, or whether both were out to prove that pigeons and chimps are as smart as people, or at least that their intelligences are not qualitatively different, we must admire the skill of both teams of investigators in teaching communication skills. But what has been called into question in these and like experiments is the use of words such as *language, symbols, sentences* to describe this kind of communication. Investigators such as Terrace and Sebeok have shown that such communication does not bear the test of language in the human sense, e.g., having a rule-governed syntax. One of the weaknesses of semiotics is the all-too-frequent use of words like *language* and *sentence* in a loose analogical sense.

This argument aside, what matters here is that these communications in Skinner's pigeons and the Rumbaughs' chimps can be understood perfectly well by Peirce's familiar dyadic model, as a sequence of interactions or dyads:

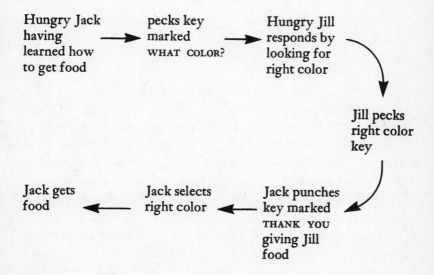

DIAGRAM 6

This sequence can of course be broken down into smaller dyads, e.g., interactions between Jack's conditioned neurones, electrical discharges along the efferent nerves leading to Jack's pecking muscles, and so on.

An African gray parrot named Alex at Purdue University has been taught to call forty objects by name, identify five colors, and distinguish between a square, a triangle, and a pentagon. When he wants to return to his cage, he says, "Wanna go back."

Many people, including some scientists, like to speak of the "language" of the Rumbaugh's chimp, Skinner's pigeons, and the Purdue parrot, to say nothing of the song of the humpback whale. These communications, however, bear little if any resemblance to human language. The former can be understood as dyadic events not qualitatively different, albeit much more complex, from other dyadic events in the Cosmos. The latter cannot be so understood.

V

Extremely recently in the history of the Cosmos, at least on the earth—perhaps less than 100,000 years ago, perhaps more—there occurred an event different in kind from all preceding events in the Cosmos. It cannot be understood as a dyadic interaction or a complexus of dyadic interactions.

It has been called variously triadic behavior, thirdness, the Delta factor, man's discovery of the sign (including symbols, language, art).

This phenomenon occurred in the evolution of man. It may have occurred elsewhere in the Cosmos, or it may have occurred in other creatures on earth. We do not know. But it is not known to have occurred elsewhere in the Cosmos and it has not been proved—despite heroic attempts with chimps, gorillas, and dolphins—to have occurred in other earth species.

The present argument does not require that triadic behavior be unique in man. Perhaps it is not. Semiotics proposes only that where triadic behavior occurs, certain new properties and relationships also come into existence.

Triadic behavior is that event in which sign *A* is understood by organism *B*, not as a signal to flee or approach, but as "meaning" or referring to another perceived segment of the environment:

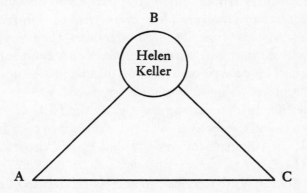

B

Helen
Keller

A   C

Signifier (*signifiant*):
W-A-T-E-R spelled in
her hand by Miss Sullivan

Referent (*signifié*):
perceived liquid flowing
over other hand

Relations AB, BC, AC cannot be explained as dyadic interactions.
This is a triadic event.

DIAGRAM 7

This triad is irreducible. That is to say, it cannot be understood as a sequence of dyads, as could the events, say, when Miss Sullivan spelled C-A-K-E into Helen's hand and Helen went to look for cake—like one of Skinner's pigeons.

At any rate, a triadic event has occurred and it is unprecedented in the Cosmos. *Thus, there is a sense in which it can be said that, given two mammals extraordinarily similar in organic structure and genetic code, and given that one species has made the breakthrough into triadic behavior and the other has not, there is, semiotically speaking, more difference between the two than there is between the dyadic animal and the planet Saturn.*

Certain new properties appear. For example, all such triadic behavior is *social* in origin. A signal received by an organism is like other signals or stimuli from its environment. But a sign requires a sign-giver. Thus, every triad of sign-reception requires another triad of sign-utterance. (See page 97.) Whether the sign is a word, a painting, or a symphony—or Robinson Crusoe writing a journal to himself—a sign transaction requires a sign-utterer and a sign-receiver.

Other new properties appear, such as the relation between the utterer and the receiver, which are subject to such familiar variables as "intersubjectivity" (I-thou) and "depersonalization" (I-it).

A particularly mysterious property is the relation between the sign (signifier) and the referent (signified). It is expressed by the troublesome copula "is," when Helen said that the perceived liquid "is" water (the word). It "is" but then again it is not. Herein surely is the root of all the troubles Stuart Chase spoke of when he said that his cat had no dealings with such a relationship and therefore was smarter or at least saner than humans.

Another unique property of the sign-user, of special significance here, is that as soon as he crosses the triadic threshold, he not only continues to exist in an environment but also has a *world*.

The *world* of the sign-user is not identical to its environment or the Cosmos.

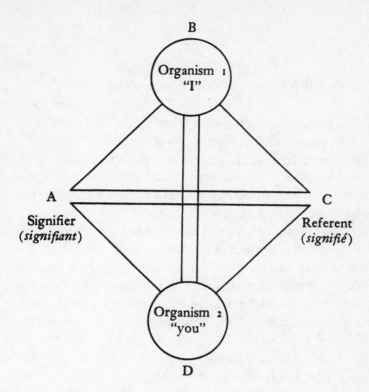

Relation AC—your giving a name to a class of objects to make a sign, and my understanding or misunderstanding of such a naming —cannot be understood as a dyadic interaction.

Relation BD—the I-you intersubjectivity of an exchange of signs —cannot be understood as a dyadic interaction.

These are two conjoined triadic events which always happen in any exchange of signs, whether in talk, looking at a painting, reading a novel, or listening to music. It allows for such peculiar properties of triadic events as understanding, misunderstanding, truth-telling, lying.

DIAGRAM 8

VI

The first Edenic world of the sign-user

Miss Sullivan (writing of Helen Keller): As the cold water gushed forth, filling the mug, I spelled "w-a-t-e-r" in Helen's free hand. The word coming so close upon the sensation of cold water rushing over her hand seemed to startle her. She dropped the mug and stood as one transfixed. A new light came into her face. She spelled "w-a-t-e-r" several times. Then she dropped on the ground and asked for its name and pointed to the pump and the trellis, and suddenly turning around asked for my name. I spelled, "Teacher." Just then the nurse brought Helen's little sister into the pump-house, and Helen spelled "baby" and pointed to the nurse. All the way back to the house she was highly excited, *and learned the name of every object she touched*, so that in a few hours she added thirty new words to her vocabulary. Here are some of them: *Door, open, shut, give, go, come,* and a great many more.*

Roger Brown and Ursula Bellugi (writing in "Three Processes in the Child's Acquisition of Syntax"): Some time in the second six months of life most children say a first intelligible word. A few months later most children are saying many words and some children go about the house all day long naming things (*table, doggie, ball,* etc.) and actions (*play, see drop,* etc.)†

---

* *Helen Keller, The Story of My Life* (New York: Airmont Publishing Co., 1965), p. 187.
† *New Directions in the Study of Language,* ed. Eric. H. Lenneberg (Cambridge: The M.I.T. Press, 1964), p. 131.

Philip E. L. Smith: Having inherited from more primitive ancestors large and efficient brains, as well as a serviceable technology, these new humans proceeded to make a quantum jump greater than anything seen before in a comparable length of time. In esthetics, in communication and symbols, in technology and adaptive efficiency, and perhaps in newer forms of social organization and more complex ways of viewing their fellows, these first modern men went on to effect a transformation worldwide in its impact.*

The signal-using organism has an environment.

The sign-user has an environment, but it also has a *world*.

The environment of an organism is those elements of the Cosmos which affect the organism significantly (Saturn does not) and to which the organism either is genetically coded to respond or has learned to respond. There are many gaps in an environment, i.e., there are elements which are without significant effect. A honey bee takes account of the bee dance of another bee indicating the direction and distance of a nectar source, but not of a grouse dance.

The sign-user has a world.

The world is segmented and named by language. All perceived objects and actions and qualities are named. Even the gaps are named—by the word *gaps*. An African Bushman has hundreds of names for plants which are either noxious or medicinally beneficial. But he also has a word *bush* to name all other plants. The Cosmos is accounted for willy-nilly, rightly or wrongly, mythically or scientifically, its past, present, and future. All men in all cultures know what is under the earth, what is above the earth, and where the Cosmos came from.

---

* Philip E. L. Smith in *Cro-Magnon Man*, ed. by Tom Prideaux (New York: Time-Life Books, 1973), p. 7.

The sign *Canada* is part of the world of most sign-users. It can signify whatever lies at hand to be signified, either a place and a people one knows or a large pink place on a map transected by longitudes and latitudes.

If there is an unknown territory in the heart of Africa, it is labeled as such on maps and known to sign-users as "unknown territory."

A cat has no myths and names no real or imaginary beings. It responds to the Cosmos exactly as it has learned or been programmed to respond.

For the sign-user, a world is imposed upon the Cosmos—to which he still responds like any other organism.

For example, he still responds to signals, to heat, light, hunger, sudden noises, perhaps also to female pheromones, perhaps even to the magnetic field of the earth and the gravitational attraction of the moon. But there are other segments of the Cosmos to which he does not respond, even though astrologers say he does.

The environment has gaps. But the world of the sign-user is a totality. The Cosmos is totally construed by signs, whether the signs be the myth of Tiamat, Newtonian cosmology, or through the auspices of such popular signifiers as "outer space," "out there," "the heavens," "the sky," "stars," and so on.

Not all items of an environment are part of a world. A noxious element—say, an increase in ultraviolet radiation—is a significant environmental factor and may cause skin cancer. But it is unkown to the patient and not part of his world. But the signs *unicorn* and *boogerman* may be very much a part of a person's world and yet have no known counterpart in the Cosmos.

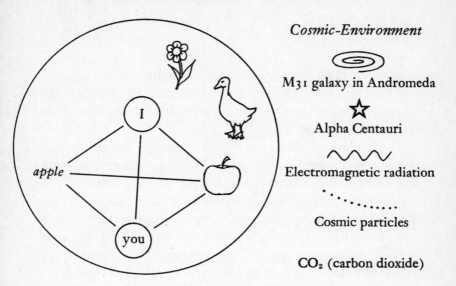

Cosmic-Environment

M31 galaxy in Andromeda

Alpha Centauri

Electromagnetic radiation

Cosmic particles

CO_2 (carbon dioxide)

The Strange World of the Triadic Creature

Note some odd things about the self's world. One is that it is not the same as the Cosmos-environment. The planet Venus may be a sign in the self's world as the evening star or the morning star, but the galaxy M31 may not be present at all. Another oddity is that the self's world contains things which have no counterpart in the Cosmos, such as centaurs, Big Foot, détente, World War I (which is past), World War III (which may not occur). Yet another odd thing is that the word *apple* which you utter is part of my world but it is not a singular thing like an individual apple. It is in fact understandable only insofar as it conforms to a rule for uttering *apples*. But the oddest thing of all is your status in my world. You—Betty, Dick—are like other items in my world— cats, dogs, and apples. But you have a unique property. You are also co-namer, co-discoverer, co-sustainer of my world—whether you are Kafka whom I read or Betty who reads this. Without you—Franz, Betty—I would have no world.

DIAGRAM 9

VII

The world of the sign-user is a world of signs.

The sign, as Saussure said, is a union of signifier (the sound-image of a word) and signified (the concept of an object, action, quality).

If you protest that your world does not consist of signs but rather of apples and trees and people and stars and walking and yellow, Saussure might reply that you don't know any of these things but only a sensory input which your brain encodes as a percept, then abstracts as a concept which is in turn encoded and "known" under the auspices of language.

Take the sign *apple*. It consists both of the sound-image *apple* and also of a kind of general impression of apples you have known, embodying qualities of roundedness, redness, shine, texture, and sound of apple flesh at bite and pop of apple-skin against teeth, tart-tang taste, and so on.*

One's world is thus segmented by an almost unlimited number of signs, signifying not only here-and-now things

---

* I will not try to decide here whether what the word *apple* conjures up in your mind, its *signifié*, is a percept or a concept, because it is somewhere in between. A percept refers to an individual apple. A concept is an abstraction from all apples, a definition of *apple*. But the *signifié* of *apple* is both and neither. What comes to mind when I hear *apple*, what in fact the word articulates within itself, is neither an individual apple nor a definition of *apple* but a quality of appleness, such as John Cheever intended in his title, *World of Apples*. Perhaps it should be called a "concrete concept" or an "abstract percept," or what Gerard Manley Hopkins called *inscape*.

Let us take note of a notorious philosophical farrago without attempting to resolve it: Why is it that when we look at an apple, we believe we are looking at an apple out there, and not at a sensory impression, a picture, in our brain? This puzzle can hardly be addressed here, since it is nothing less than the main source of the troubles which have dogged solipsist philosophers from Descartes and Locke to the present day. My own conviction is that semiotics provides an escape from the solipsist prison by its stress on the social origins of language—you have to point to an apple and name it for me before I know there is such a thing—and the existence of a world of apples outside ourselves.

and qualities and actions but also real and imaginary objects in the past and future. If I wish to catalogue my world, I could begin with a free association which could go on for months: *desk, pencil, writing, itch, Saussure, Belgian, minority, war, the end of the world, Superman, Birmingham, flying, slithy toves, General Grant, the 1984 Olympics, Lilliput, Mozart, Don Giovanni, The Grateful Dead, backing and filling, say it isn't so, dreaming* . . .

The nearest thing to a recorded world of signs is the world of H. C. Earwicker in Joyce's *Finnegans Wake.*

VIII

In a sign, the signifier and the signified are interpenetrated so that the signifier becomes, in a sense, transformed by the signified.

Saussure gave a formal analysis of the dual nature of the sign. It remained for Werner and Kaplan and other writers to describe the dynamic process by which the signifier and signified are interpenetrated and the former transformed.

If you do not believe that the word *apple* has been transformed by the percept *apple*, do this experiment: repeat the word *apple* aloud fifty times. Somewhere along the way, it will suddenly lose its magic transformation into appleness and like Cinderella at midnight become the drab little vocable it really is.

Further evidence of the interpenetration of signifier and signified is false onomatopoeia.

Words like *boom, pow, tick-tock* are said to be onomatopoetic. But what about these words: *spatter, slice, brittle, limber, blue, yellow, high, low, rattle*? Many people would say that there is some resemblance between these words and the things they signify. *Blue* sounds more like blue than *yellow*. *Brittle* sounds brittler than *limber*. But there is no such resemblance. Or rather, what resemblance there is, is far more remote and problematical than it appears. The resemblance occurs because the signifier and signified have been interpenetrated through use by the sign-user.

Slimy does not sound slimy to a German speaker.

IX

Signs undergo an evolution, or rather a devolution.

At first, the signifier serves as the discovery vehicle through which the signified is known, e.g., Helen Keller discovering water through *water*—or any two-year-old learning the name of a new object—Peirce's example:

> BOY: What is that?
> FATHER: That is a balloon.

Note that when a child hears a new name, he will repeat it; his lips will move silently while he frowns and muses as he considers *how* this round inflated object can be fitted into this peculiar utterance, *balloon*.

Next, the signifier becomes transformed by the signified: the signifier *balloon* becomes informed by the distention, the stretched-rubber, light, up-tending, squinch-sound-against-fingers signified.

Next, there is a hardening and closure of the signifier, so that in the end the signified becomes encased in a simulacrum like a mummy in a mummy case.

> FIRST BIRD WATCHER: What is that?
> SECOND BIRD WATCHER: That is only a sparrow.

A devaluation has occurred. The bird itself has disappeared into the sarcophagus of its sign. The unique living creature is assigned to its class of signs, a second-class mummy in the basement collection of mummy cases.

But a recovery is possible. The signified can be recovered from the ossified signifier, sparrow from *sparrow*.

A sparrow can be recovered under conditions of catastrophe.

The German soldier in *All Quiet on the Western Front* could see an ordinary butterfly as a creature of immense beauty and value in the trenches of the Somme.

A poet can wrench signifier out of context and exhibit it in all its queerness and splendor.*

Cézanne recovered apples from the commonplace sign, *apples*.

Scientists recover the inexhaustible mystery of the signified from the mundane closed-off simulacrum of the world-sign.

One sees a line of ants crossing the sidewalk and sees it as—*ants crossing the sidewalk.* Fabre saw ants crossing the sidewalk and stopped to wonder where they came from, where they were going, how they knew how to get there, and why. Then, like von Frisch and his bees, he discovered there is no end to the mystery of ants.

X

Consciousness: *Conscious* from *con-scio*, I know with.

Consciousness is that act of attention to something under the auspices of its sign, an act which is social in its origin. What Descartes did not know: no such isolated individual as he described can be conscious.

It is no etymological accident that the prefix *con-* is part

---

* The semioticist most acutely aware of this devolution of the sign and its renewal through the "defamiliarization" of art is the Russian formalist, Victor Schklovsky.

of the word, since the origin of consciousness is the initiation of the sign-user into the world of signs by a sign-giver.

It is also not an accident that grammatical usage requires that *conscious* and *consciousness* are generally followed by *of*. One is always conscious *of* something.

It is also the case that one is always conscious *of* something *as* something—its sign.

If a hunter is conscious of an animal in the field, it is part of the act of consciousness to *place* it—as a rabbit, fox, deer. The signing process tends to configure segments of the Cosmos under the auspices of a sign, often mistakenly. It is often possible to *see* a certain pattern of light and shadow *as* a rabbit, ears, and all. The hunter coming closer may say with surprise: "I thought it was a rabbit."

Deer hunters, who are increasingly shooting each other more often than deer, invariably report: "But I *saw* a deer!"

XI

If the sign-user first enters into an Edenic state by virtue of his discovery and constitution of the world by signs, like Helen Keller or any normal two-year-old, and if aboriginal sign-use is a joyful concelebration of the world through an utterance in which the ancient environment of the Cosmos is transformed and beheld in common through the magic prism of the sign, it is also, semiotically speaking, an Eden which harbors its own semiotic snake in the grass.

The fateful flaw of human semiotics is this: that of all the objects in the entire Cosmos which the sign-user can apprehend through the conjoining of signifier and signified (word uttered and thing beheld), there is one which forever escapes his comprehension—and that is the sign-user himself.

Semiotically, the self is literally unspeakable to itself. One cannot speak or hear a word which signifies oneself, as one can speak or hear a word signifying anything else, e.g., *apple, Canada*, 7-*Up*.

The self of the sign-user can never be grasped, because, once the self locates itself at the dead center of its world, there is no signified to which a signifier can be joined to make a sign. The self has no sign of itself. No signifier applies. All signifiers apply equally.

You are *Ralph* to me and I am *Walker* to you, but you are not *Ralph* to you and I am not *Walker* to me. (Have you ever wondered why the Ralphs you know look as if they ought to be called Ralph and not Robert?)

For me, certain signifiers fit you, and not others. For me, all signifiers fit me, one as well as another. I am rascal, hero, craven, brave, treacherous, loyal, at once the secret hero and asshole of the Cosmos.

You are not a sign in your world. Unlike the other signifiers in your world which form more or less stable units with the perceived world-things they signify, the signifier of yourself is mobile, freed up, and operating on a sliding semiotic scale from $- \propto$ to $\propto$.

The signified of the self is semiotically loose and caroms around the Cosmos like an unguided missile.

From the moment the signifying self turned inward and became conscious of itself, trouble began as the sparks flew up.

No one knows how such a state of affairs came to pass, except through the wisdom (or folly) of religion and myth.*

---

* Does ontogenesis shed any light here?

The two-year-old comes bursting into the world of signs like a child on Christmas morning. There are goodies everywhere. For him, signifying the signified is like unwrapping a gift.

What about a four-year-old? By now he should be a sovereign and native resident of his world, concelebrant with his family, at home in Eden. Listen to Gesell and his colleagues describe him: "The typical 4-year-old

But, semiotically speaking, it is possible to describe the consequences.

As a consequence of the unprecedented appearance of the triad in the Cosmos, there appeared for the first time in fifteen billion years (as far as we know) a creature which is ashamed of itself and which seeks cover in myriad disguises.

One semioticist defined the subject of his study as the only organism which tells lies.

The exile from Eden is, semiotically, the banishment of the self-conscious self from its own world of signs.

The banquet is still there, but it is Banquo in attendance.

The self perceives itself as naked. Every self is ashamed of itself.

The semiotic history of this creature thereafter could be written in terms of the successive attempts, both heroic and absurd, of the signifying creature to escape its nakedness and to find a permanent semiotic habiliment for itself—often by identifying itself with other creatures in its world.

. . . tends to be rather a joy. His enthusiasm, his exuberance, his willingness to go more than halfway to meet others in a spirit of fun are all extremely refreshing . . . He is basically highly positive, enthusiastic, appreciative. This makes him fun to be with, an engaging, amusing, ever-challenging friend. You have to be on your toes to keep up with spirited, fanciful FOUR, but at least you have an even chance of success . . . With other children, things as a rule go rather well. FOURS enjoy each other; they appreciate the challenge that other children offer. This is an age at which children interest and admire each other most . . ." [Louise Bates Ames et al., *The Gesell Institute's Child from One to Six* (New York: Harper and Row, 1979).]

The four-year-old is a concelebrant of the world and even of his own peers.

The seven-year-old? Something has happened in the interval.

"More aware of and withdrawn into self . . . Seems to be in 'another world' . . . Self-conscious about own body. Sensitive about exposing body. Does not like to be touched. Modest about toileting . . . Protects self by withdrawal. May be unwilling to expose knowledge, for fear of being laughed at or criticized . . . Apt to expect too much of self." [Arnold Gesell and Frances Ilg, *The Child from Five to Ten* (New York: Harper and Row, 1946).]

Among Alaskan Indians, this practice is called totemism. In the Western world, it is called role-modeling.

The question must arise: What is the nature of the catastrophe of the self? Is the catastrophe nothing more or less than the breakthrough itself, the sudden emergence of the triadic organism into a dyadic world? And is the predicament of the self the price of naming and knowing? Or is the catastrophe a subsequent event, a bad move in the exercise of its freedom by the sign-user? Is it a turning from the concelebration of the world to a solitary absorption with self?

It is fruitful to speculate on the possible nature of other intelligences (ETIs) in the Cosmos, if they exist.

Presumably, they too have achieved the triadic breakthrough. Might they not have achieved the world of signs without succumbing to the terrible penalty? Might there not exist preternatural intelligences who do not necessarily share the shadow-life of the earth-self?

Much of current speculation about the nature of ETIs— what level of technology have you achieved?, etc.—is misguided. The first question an earthling should ask of an ETI is not: What is the level of your science? but rather: Did it also happen to you? Do you have a self? If so, how do you handle it? Did you suffer a catastrophe?

XII

As soon as the self becomes self-conscious—that is, aware of its own unique unformulability in its world of signs— from that moment forward, it cannot escape the predicament of its placement in the world.

An organism exists in its environment in only one mode, that of an open system responding to those segments of its

environment to which it is genetically programmed to respond or to which it has learned to respond.

But a self must be *placed* in a world. It cannot *not* be
placed. If it chooses by default not to be placed, then its
placement is that of not choosing to be placed.

Some Traditional Modes of Self-Placement:

(*a*) Totemistic.

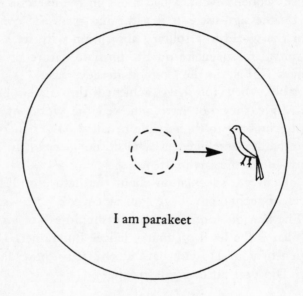

I am parakeet

DIAGRAM 10

The self, here drawn as a dotted circle because it is problematical to itself, finds its identity in one or another of the
resplendent signs of its world, especially those possessed of
those qualities most admired by the self: animals, trees, clouds,
thunder, sky, falcon.

QUESTION: What are you?
ALEUT INDIAN: I am bear.

QUESTION: What are you?
MOVIE ACTRESS: I'm a Leo.

(*b*) Eastern Pantheistic. The self is identified with God, the God which is everywhere in the world, including one's self, yet behind the illusory appearances of world-signs. Therefore, God is to be found in the true depths of the self.

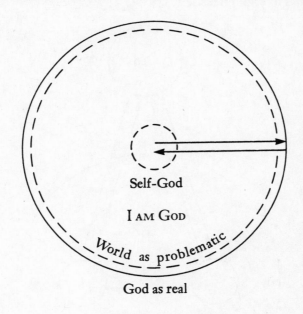

DIAGRAM II

Both the world and the self are problematical. The self becomes itself by identifying with God, who is found both in one's self and behind the *maya* of the world.

Who are you?

I am *Atman*, which is to say God in myself, but also *Brahman*, the God of the Cosmos.

(*c*) Theistic-historical (Judaism, Christianity, Islam). The self becomes itself by recognizing God as a spirit, creator of the Cosmos and therefore of one's self as a creature, a wounded creature but a creature nonetheless, who shares with a community of like creatures the belief that God, who transcends the entire Cosmos and has actually entered human history— or will enter it—in order to redeem man from the catastrophe which has overtaken his self.

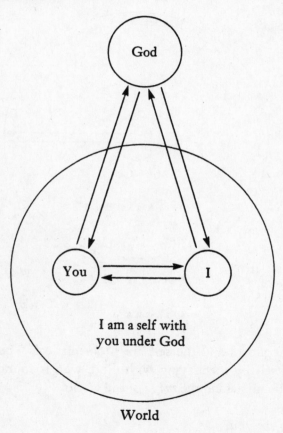

DIAGRAM 12

XIII

In a post-religious technological society, these traditional resources of the self are no longer available, leaving in general only the two options: self conceived as immanent, consumer of the techniques, goods, and services of society; or as transcendent, a member of the transcending community of science and art.

(*a*) Self as Immanent. The self sees itself as an immanent being in the world, existing in a mode of being often conceived on the model of organism-in-an-environment as a consequence of the powerful credentials of science and technology.

Such immanence is a continuum. At one end: the compliant role-player and consumer and holder of a meaningless job, the anonymous "one"—German *man*—in a mass society, whether a backfence gossip* or an Archie Bunker beer-drinking TV-watcher.

At the other end: the "autonomous self," who is savvy to all the techniques of society and appropriates them according to his or her discriminating tastes, whether it be learning "parenting skills," consciousness-raising, consumer advocacy, political activism liberal or conservative, saving whales, TM, TA, ACLU, New Right, square-dancing, creative cooking, moving out to country, moving back to central city, etc.

The self is still problematical to itself, but it solves its predicament of placement vis-à-vis the world either by a passive consumership or by a discriminating transaction with the world and with informed interactions with other selves.

---

* Here might be listed all the "existentialia" of Heidegger, the inauthentic ways in which the *Dasein*, or self, inserts itself into its world, e.g., *Gerede*, talk, gossip; *Neugier*, curiosity.

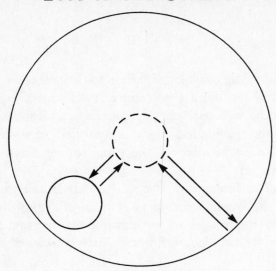

The Immanent Self feeling somewhat Problematical and therefore staking everything on Interactions with other Selves and with the World

Interactions with other selves: more or less successful; that is, at one pole, exploitative, manipulative, etc.; at other pole, caring, creative, imaginative, venturesome, etc.

Interaction with world: more or less successful; that is, at one pole, passive consumership of TV, food, drugs, etc.; at other pole, discriminating consumership of do-it-yourself hobbies, participatory sports, gourmet cooking, off-beaten-track travel to Katmandu, etc.

DIAGRAM 13

(*b*) Self as Transcendent. In a post-religious age, the only transcendence open to the self is self-transcendence, that is, the transcending of the world by the self. The available modes of transcendence in such an age are science and art.

(*i*) Transcendence by Science. The scientist is the prince and sovereign of the age. His transcendence of the world is genuine. That is to say, he stands in a posture of objectivity over against the world, a world which he sees as a series of specimens or exemplars, and interactions, energy exchanges, secondary causes—in a word: dyadic events. (See diagram 14, page 116.)

The problematical self, like the young Einstein who couldn't stand the dreariness of everyday life, discovers science and transcends the world. In orbit, he enters an elect community of other scientists, however small, to whom he can address sentences about the world.

The scientist, though transcendent and "in orbit" around the ordinary world, has minimal problems with reentry. That is to say, he is able to maintain a more or less stable orbit so that in ordinary intercourse he is generally seen as no more than "absentminded," like Einstein, who thought for twenty years about his general theory, and von Frisch, who pondered bee communication for forty years.

Reentry problems become noticeable in less inspired scientists. The divorced wife of an astronomer at the Mount Wilson Observatory accused her husband of "angelism-bestialism." He was so absorbed in his work, the search for the quasar with the greatest red shift, that when he came home to his pleasant subdivision house, he seemed to take his pleasure like a god descending from Olympus into the world of mortals, ate heartily, had frequent intercourse with his wife, watched TV, read Mickey Spillane, and said not a word to wife or children.

But at the peak periods of scientific transcendence, he, the scientist, becomes the secular saint of the age: Einstein is still referred to as a benign deity.

With the waning of transcendence, reentry problems in-

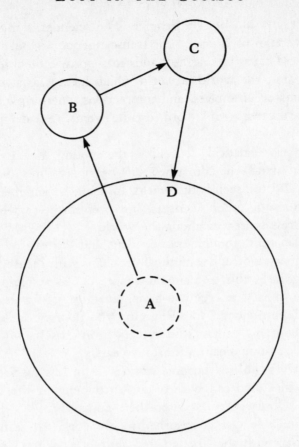

How the Problematical Self can Escape its Predicament by Science

AB = The problematical self, finding itself in a disappointing world and in all manner of difficult relationships, escapes by joining the scientific community, either by becoming a scientist or by understanding science.

BC = The transcending community of scientists.

CD = From the perspective of BC, the world can now be seen by A triumphantly as a dyadic system.

Diagram 14

crease. One manifestation, which always amazes laymen, is the jealousy and lack of scruple of scientists. Their anxiety to receive credit often seems more appropriate to used-car salesmen than to a transcending community.

Other examples of reentry failures: the general fatuity of scientists in political matters, their naïveté and credulity before tricksters. The magician Randi says that scientists are easier to fool—e.g., by Uri Geller—than are children.

More distressing consequences occur when the zeal and excitement of a scientific community runs counter to the interests of the world community, e.g., when scientists at Los Alamos did not oppose the bomb drop over Hiroshima and Nagasaki. The joys of science and the joys of life as a human are not necessarily convergent. As Freeman Dyson put it, the "sin" of the scientists at Los Alamos was not that they made the bomb but that they enjoyed it so much.

(*ii*) Decayed Orbits of Transcendence. The layman can in some cases participate in the transcendent community of science, but often at a price.

Consider a familiar example, the lay Freudian, that is, the avid reader and disciple of Freud who does, in a degree, share in the excitement of Freud's insights but whose excitement all too often derives not from a shared discovery but from the sense of election to an elite from which vantage point one can play a one-upmanship game with ordinary folk: "What you say is not really what you mean. What you really mean, whether you know it or not, is—"

Their impoverishment is to be located in both an inflation of theory and a devaluation of the world theorized about. They out-Freud Freud without the scruples of Freud.

Yet they, the lay scientists, those who perceive themselves in the community of scientists and at some remove from the ordinary world, may be better off than those who live immanent lives, beneficiaries of science and technology, but

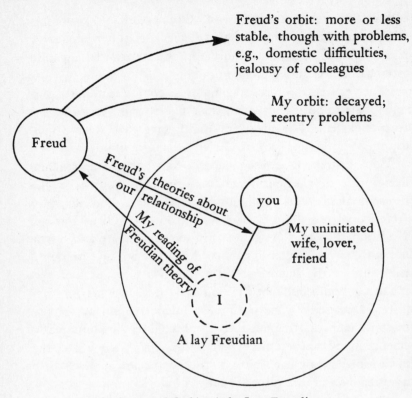

Freud's orbit: more or less
stable, though with problems,
e.g., domestic difficulties,
jealousy of colleagues

My orbit: decayed;
reentry problems

Freud

Freud's theories about
our relationship

My reading of
Freudian theory

you

My uninitiated
wife, lover,
friend

I

A lay Freudian

The Decayed Orbit of the Lay Freudian

or, How it is one thing to be Freud and to spend a life inducing
a remarkable theory from the endlessly complex manifold of
human phenomena
and, How it is something else to read some Freud, master a few
principles, return to the ordinary world and human relationships
with the sense that you alone are privy to the hidden mechanisms
of these relationships. Such reentries can be disastrous for both
parties, Freudian and non-Freudian.

DIAGRAM 15

with only a glimmering of the scientists, the glimmering that there are scientists and that "they" know about every sector of the world, including one's very self. "They" not only know about the Cosmos, they know about me, my aches and pains, my brain functions, even my neuroses. A remarkable feature of the secondhand knowledge of scientific transcendence is the attribution of omniscience to "them." "They" know.

They are expected to know. Example: a recent Donahue Show in which paraplegics discussed their troubles. The message: rage at doctors. "They" could cure us if they wanted to, took the time, did their research. The powers attributed to *them*, the scientists—powers which they, the scientists, never claimed—are as magical as those of the old gods.

The layman, dazzled by the extraordinary accomplishments of science and technology, nevertheless gives away too much to science. Where the genuine scientist is generally amazed at the meagerness of knowledge in his own field, the layman is apt to assign omniscience as what he takes to be a property of scientific transcendence.

(*iii*) Transcendence by Art. If the scientist is the prince of the post-religious age, lord and sovereign of the Cosmos itself through his transcendence of it, the artist is the suffering servant of the age, who, through his own transcendence and his naming of the predicaments of the self, becomes rescuer and savior not merely to his fellow artists but to his fellow sufferers. Like the scientists, he transcends in his use of signs. Unlike the scientists, he speaks not merely to a small community of fellow artists but to the world of men who understand him.

It is no accident that, for the past hundred years or so, the artist (poet, novelist, painter, dramatist) has registered a dissent from the modern proposition that, with the advance of

science and technology, man's lot will improve in direct proportion. The alienation of the artist puzzles many, both the
scientists and technologists who are happy and busy and their
lay beneficiaries who are happy in the immanence of consumption. Most Danes and Japanese don't appear to be alienated—though there are those who say that their oblivious-
ness of their own immanence is the worst alienation of all. To
most of the happy von Frisches and Rutherfords and to the
contented denizens of Silicon Valley, the dark views of modern life held by most serious novelists since Tolstoy, most
poets since Tennyson, most painters since Millet, most dra-
matists since Schiller, have seemed neurotic indulgences. It is
possible, however, that the artist is both thin-skinned and
prophetic and, like the canary lowered into the mine shaft
to test the air, has caught a whiff of something lethal. Indeed,
as this dreadful century wears on, even the most immanent
Dane and the most proficient IBM computer-engineer is beginning to sense that all is not well, that the self can be as
desperately stranded in the transcendence of theory as in the
immanence of consumption.

The artist, caught in the predicament of the self, is at once
more vulnerable to the predicament of self than the non-
artist and at the same time privileged to escape it by the
transcendence of his art. He serves others who share his
predicament by naming it.

The difference between Einstein and Kafka, both sons of
middle-class middle-European families, both of whom found
life in the ordinary world intolerably dreary:

Einstein escaped the world by science, that is, by transcending not only the world but the Cosmos itself.

Kafka also escaped his predicament—occasionally—not by
science but by art, that is, by *seeing* and naming what had
heretofore been unspeakable, the predicament of the self in
the modern world.

The salvation of art derives in the best of modern times from a celebration of the triumph of the autonomous self—as in Beethoven's Ninth Symphony—and in the worst of times from naming the unspeakable: the strange and feckless movements of the self trying to escape itself.

Exhilaration comes from naming the unnamable and hearing it named.

If Kafka's *Metamorphosis* is presently a more accurate account of the self than Beethoven's Ninth Symphony, it is the more exhilarating for being so.

The naming of the predicament of the self by art is its reversal. Hence the salvific effect of art. Through art, the predicament of self becomes not only speakable but laughable. Helen Keller and any two-year-old and Kafka's friends laughed when the unnamable was named. Kafka and his friends laughed when he read his stories to them.

The community of art is not the elect community of science but the community of the artist and all who share his predicament and who can understand his signs.

The impoverishment? It comes from the transience of the salvation of art, both for the maker of the sign (the artist) and for the receiver of the sign.

The self in its predicament is exhilarated in both the making and the receiving of a sign—for a while.

After a while, both the artist and the self which receives the sign are back in the same fix or worse—because both have had a taste of transcendence and community.

If poets often commit suicide, it is not because their poems are bad but because they are good. Whoever heard of a bad poet committing suicide? The reader is only a little better off. The exhilaration of a good poem lasts twenty minutes, an hour at most.

Unlike the scientist, the artist has reentry problems that are frequent and catastrophic.

In fact, a catalogue of the spectacular reentries and flame-outs of the artist is nothing other than a pathology of the self in the twentieth century, much as the fits and frenzies of Saint Vitus's Dance were signs of the ills of an earlier age.

What account, then, can a semiotic give of the paradoxical impoverishments and enrichments of the self in the present age?

Why do people often feel bad in good environments and good in bad environments? Why did Mother Teresa think that affluent Westerners often seemed poorer than the Calcutta poor, the poorest of the poor?

The paradox comes to pass because the impoverishments and enrichments of a *self* in a *world* are not necessarily the same as the impoverishments and enrichments of an *organism* in an *environment.*

The organism is needy or not needy accordingly as needs are satisfied or not satisfied by its environment.

The self in a world is rich or poor accordingly as it succeeds in identifying its otherwise unspeakable self, e.g., mythically, by identifying itself with a world-sign, such as a totem; religiously, by identifying itself as a creature of God.

But totemism doesn't work in a scientific age because no one believes, no matter how hard he tries, that he can "become" a tiger or a parakeet. Cf. the depression of a Princeton tiger or Yale bulldog, one hour after the game.

In a post-religious age, the only recourses of the self are self as transcendent and self as immanent.

The impoverishment of the immanent self derives from a perceived loss of sovereignty to "them," the transcending scientists and experts of society. As a consequence, the self sees its only recourse as an endless round of work, diversion, and consumption of goods and services. Failing this and having some inkling of its plight, it sees no way out because it has come to see itself as an organism in an environment and

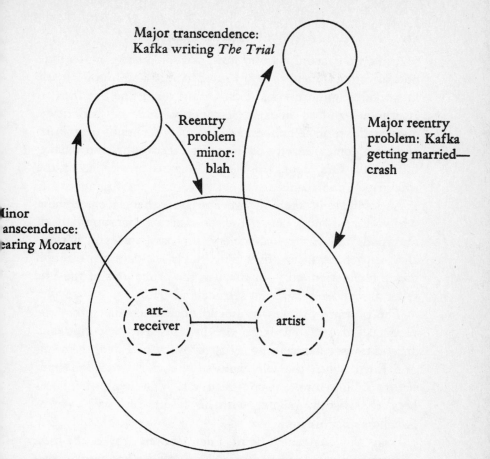

Major transcendence:
Kafka writing *The Trial*

Reentry
problem
minor:
blah

Major reentry
problem: Kafka
getting married—
crash

Minor
transcendence:
hearing Mozart

art-
receiver

artist

Different Reentry Problems of Artist and Art-Receiver: Mainly Quantitative

It is one thing to write *The Sound and the Fury*, to achieve the artistic transcendence of discerning meaning in the madness of the twentieth century, then to finish it, then to find oneself at Reed's drugstore the next morning. A major problem of reentry, not solved but anaesthetized by alcohol.

It is something else to listen to a superb performance of Mozart's Twenty-first Piano Concerto, to come to the end of it, to walk out into Columbus Circle afterwards. At best, a moderately sustained exaltation; at worst, a mild letdown.

DIAGRAM 16

so can't understand why it feels so bad in the best of all possible environments—say, a good family and a good home in a good neighborhood in East Orange on a fine Wednesday afternoon—and so finds itself secretly relishing bad news, assassinations, plane crashes, and the misfortunes of neighbors, and even comes secretly to hope for catastrophe, earthquake, hurricane, wars, apocalypse—anything to break out of the iron grip of immanence.

Enrichment in such an age appears either as enrichment within immanence, i.e., the discriminating consumption of the goods and services of society, such as courses in personality enrichment, creative play, and self-growth through group interaction, etc.—or through the prime joys of the age, self-transcendence through science and art.

The pleasure of such transcendence derives not from the recovery of self but from the loss of self. Scientific and artistic transcendence is a partial recovery of Eden, the semiotic Eden, when the self explored the world through signs before falling into self-consciousness. Von Frisch with his bees, the Lascaux painter with his bison were as happy as Adam naming his animals.

I say "partial recovery of Eden" because even the best scientist and artist must reenter the world he has transcended and there's the rub: the spectacular miseries of reentry— especially when the transcendence is so exalted as to be not merely Adam-like but godlike.

It is difficult for gods to walk the earth without taking the forms of beasts.

It is even more difficult for one god to get along with another god. Freud not only could not get along with the Jewish God but frothed and fell out when rivaled by a fellow transcender like Carl Jung.

Two gods in the Cosmos is one too many.

Thus, transcendence, like immanence, has its own scale of enrichment and impoverishment.

Question: In the light of the above description of the semiotic predicament of the self—its unspeakableness in a world of signs—and in the light of the need of the self to become a self and, under the exigency of truth, to become its own self, that and no other—and in the light of the forces of impoverishment and enrichment as well as self-deception, which of the following self-identities would strike you as being (1) the most impoverished, (2) the most enriched?

(*a*) An Archie Bunker type who lives in Queens

(*b*) A mathematical physicist working as a fellow at the Institute for Advanced Study at Princeton

(*c*) An Alabama Baptist

(*d*) A New York novelist removed to a pre-revolutionary Connecticut farmhouse where he is living with his fifth wife

(*e*) A Japanese Zen master recently removed from Kyoto to La Jolla

(*f*) An American Zen postulant recently removed from Chicago to Kyoto

(*g*) A Dublin Catholic

(*h*) A Belfast Protestant

(*i*) A housewife who watches five hours of soap opera a day

(*j*) A housewife who attends a well-run consciousness-raising group

(*k*) A member of the Tasaday tribe in the Philippines before its discovery by the white man

(*l*) A Virginia Episcopalian

(*m*) An Orthodox Jew

(*n*) An unbelieving Ethical Culture Jew

(*o*) A Southern poet who has sex with his students

(*p*) A homosexual poet who calls himself a "flaming fag"

(*q*) A homosexual accountant who practices in the closet

(*r*) A four-year-old child

(*s*) A seven-year-old child

(*t*) A twelve-year-old child

(*u*) An Atlanta junior executive who fancies he looks like Tom Selleck, dresses Western, and frequents singles bars

(*v*) A housewife who becomes fed up, walks out, and commits herself totally to NOW

(*w*) A housewife who sticks out a bad marriage

(*x*) A New Rochelle commuter who quits the rat race, buys a ketch, and sails for the Leeward Islands

(*y*) A New York woman novelist who writes dirty books but is quite conventional in her behavior

(*z*) A Southern woman novelist who writes conventional novels of manners and who fornicates at every opportunity

(*aa*) A Texan

(*bb*) A KGB *apparatchik*

(*cc*) A white planter in Mississippi

(*dd*) A black sharecropper in Mississippi

(*ee*) A Fourth Degree Knight of Columbus

(*ff*) None of the above, for reason of the fact that, whatever the impoverishing and enriching forces, it is impossible so to categorize an individual self—except possibly (*r*) and (*bb*), but even there, one cannot be sure. As anyone knows, a person chosen from any of the above classes may turn out against all expectations to be either a total loss as a person or that most remarkable of phenomena, an intact human self

(CHECK ONE OR MORE)

(13) THE TRANSCENDING SELF: *How the Self Characteristically Places itself vis-à-vis the World, particularly through modes of Transcendence and Immanence*

SCENE: A Corn Dance at the Taos Indian pueblo in the 1940s. There has been a long dry spell. The dancers invoke the kachinas (god-ancestors) of the West who will come at the winter solstice and leave at the summer solstice. The dancers supplicate the kachinas by a monotonous and rhythmic pounding of bare feet on the hard-packed earth.

It is not a notable festival. There is not much masking or face- and body-painting, nor any sign of the flamboyant buffalo and deer totemism of the hunting dances. The costumes are dark, drab kilts. The dance itself is perfunctory, more light-footed and syncopated than most Pueblo dances.

But it is a magical place.

Over there is the squat adobe church of San Francisco de Ranchos de Taos. But here in the vast open plaza there is also the sense of the mysteries conducted within the old Great Kiva, of which hardly a trace remains.

The setting sun is already reddening the upper slopes of the Sangre de Cristo Mountains. Not far away, nestled in the pines of the same Blood-of-Christ Mountains is a small shrine commemorating D. H. Lawrence, with a monstrance purporting to contain his ashes. Atop the shrine is a queer-looking epicene eagle with breasts: Lawrence as Phoenix rising from the ashes.

All manner of artists and writers, mystics, dropouts, and peyote-poppers live in the foothills. But a little farther north, at Los Alamos, an elite group of scientists is conducting an experiment which will fatefully alter the entire course of human history.

It is as if all the forces of the Cosmos had intersected here. The old cosmological gods remained even after the new God came. The new God remains after the transcending spirit of science and art has come. Even the old Brahman self-god of the East has lately arrived.

It is a haunted place, haunted by old gods and now by new people possessed by spirits all their own. Jungians from all over are drawn here as irresistibly as flies to pheromones, knowing that they can find in this enchanted sky-country the very incarnations of their archetypes and demons.

CAST OF CHARACTERS: Among those present at the Corn Dance are a nuclear physicist, his assistant, an old Pueblo Indian dancer, a young Pueblo Indian dancer, an English novelist, a divorcée, a tourist from Moline, Illinois, a Catholic priest, a radio repairman, a Marxist technician.

Some of the ten feel that they transcend the others. That is to say, he or she may feel that by virtue of a certain education, a certain wisdom, a certain talent, a certain gnosis, he stands in such a relation to the others that he can understand them and they can't understand him.

For example, the English novelist can perhaps be said to transcend the Illinois tourist, understand him and his camera —in fact, has written about him—in a sense in which the tourist does not understand the novelist.

The physicist and his assistant, both of whom are amateur anthropologists, profess to have an understanding of both the Indian dancers and the Catholic priest which neither the priest nor the dancers profess to have of the physicist and his assistant.

The young Indian dancer believes that he transcends the old Indian dancer because he, the young Indian, has put behind him myth and superstition for a world of science and progress.

The old Indian dancer believes that he transcends the young dancer because he, the old Indian, has kept the cosmological myths by which the world, life, and time are integrated into a meaningful whole while the deranged Western society in Albuquerque goes to pieces.

A similar symmetrical relation of transcendence exists between the physicist and the novelist. The physicist believes that science—i.e., psychology—can at least in principle explain what makes the novelist tick by taking account of his early repressions, his later sublimations, and so on. Whereas the novelist, famous for his sharp eye and his knack for sizing up people and rendering them with a few deft strokes, has already "placed" the American scientist just as he has placed the tourist and the Indians.

There are three questions to keep in mind while reading the following summary of the various modes of transcendence and immanence of the ten characters.

Question (I): Is there any sense in which it can be said truthfully that this or that member of the cast does in fact transcend some other member? Or are the ten no more or less than as described, a cast of characters, and therefore no judgment of transcending superiority or immanent inferiority can be objectively arrived at?

Question (II): But in a play it is sometimes fair to say that one character is better or worse than another. There are, after all, good people and bad people. Can you say, then, that some of the ten are better or worse than the others? If so, are the best also the most transcendent?

Question (III): Which character do you most nearly identify with? Which character would you rather be?

(*a*) A nuclear physicist: a youngish scientist, hard at work on the Manhattan Project at Los Alamos. He is having, as Freeman Dyson put it, the best time of his life, embarked as he is on a top-secret project set down in a wilderness with an elite of an elite, the best scientific brains in the Western world, even though he knows he is making a weapon which will almost certainly kill thousands of human beings and may very well spell man's ultimate self-destruction. Yet he is no narrowly educated scientist. His interests are far-ranging. He is by way of being an amateur ethnologist, a student of Oriental philosophy, and a member of a competent if unprofessional string quartet. He can speak as readily of Ramakrishna and Beethoven's last quartets as he does of Planck and Fermi.

As he watches the Corn Dance, he is engaged in an animated conversation with his assistant, a handsome blond girl. It is mostly a lecture, to which she gives her rapt attention. He compares the festivals and ceremonials of the different pueblos. Taos is rather ordinary. She ought to see the Corn Dance at Santo Domingo! On the feast day of the saint, the Catholic and tribal religions converge in a nice way characteristic of the tolerant pueblos. The statue of St. Dominic is taken from the church, paraded through the streets to the accompaniment of snare drums and gunshots, then stuck up on a cottonwood branch to enjoy the native ceremonial. In his low, earnest voice, he tells her of the pueblo equivalent of the Virgin Mary: "They call her the Spider Grandmother or Thought Woman, who created all things by thinking them into existence. Rather nice, don't you think?"

"Oh yes! Oh yes!" murmurs his assistant, leaning toward him.

(*b*) His assistant, a tall striking blonde, a graduate student from Berkeley who shares the scientist's every interest but one: she is deeply and frantically in love with him and therefore is both miserable for fear he may not love her and also ecstatically transcendent toward the crowd of tourists, feeling sorry for them not only because they have been transcended but also because they are not in love.

(c) An old Pueblo Indian dancer, who has never left the pueblo, who believes the cosmological myths of the pueblo and who further believes that the Corn Dance will invoke the kachinas of the West and that rain will come to the parched fields in consequence.

(d) A young Pueblo Indian dancer, a sophomore at the University of New Mexico in Albuquerque, a major in business administration, a promising basketball forward, for whom it goes without saying that the cosmological myths of his tribe are just that, myths, to be taken no more seriously than what he considers the Judaeo-Christian myths of the Catholic Church in which he was baptized. He joined the Newman Club at U. of N.M. to meet girls and did. It is with a complex good-natured irony that he paints his body and dons the costume and enters into the Corn Dance, an irony compounded of a gentle forbearance toward his elders and a sardonic contempt for the camera-clicking Anglos and tourists. He can also use the money he'll make from the photography fees.

The young dancer feels that he transcends the old dancer. He sees into the old man's credulity and the superstitious absurdity of the myth and rites of the rain god.

The old dancer is no less certain that he transcends the young dancer because the young Indian has left an intact society in which life and time and place are given meaning by belief for the deranged world of the latter-day Americans who clearly do not know who they are or what they are doing.

The scientist understands both and thinks that each is right in his own way. He sees the psychological "truth" of the cosmological myths of the old dancer. He sees the value of the skepticism of the young dancer. So he, the scientist, attempts the difficult feat of having it both ways—of not really believing in the kachinas of the West but of extracting the psychological value of the rite nevertheless.

(*e*) The English novelist settled here in Taos after sojourns in Italy and Mexico. His pallor and frailty—he looks for all the world like a non-conformist minister from his native Midlands—contrast with his writings, which celebrate savage good health, sexuality, and the dark gods of the blood. Self-contradicted or not, he has a miraculous eye for seeing into things, getting the hang of things, getting a fix on people. For him, no more than a single glance is needed to size up everyone here: the young Indian dancer with a quite conscious irony written on his Oriental-Pueblo face, as well as a deeper, darker inscrutability which he, the dancer, is not even aware of. He sees into the scientist and his girlfriend and their somewhat naïve, even callow, American lordliness—they think they're the god and goddess of a new world, what with their secret science and their secret sidelong looks at each other, each with arms folded so that his fingers can touch hers.

(*f*) A divorcée from Westchester. Still young, her face ravaged by something other than years, she has left the dim sorrowful East and a sorrowful marriage for the bright clean sunlit purity of the desert. It seems to her that her very self has been transformed by the crystalline air, the rosy light of sunset on the Sangre de Cristo range, the tang of piñon smoke in the evenings. Surely she has come to the right place! She paints, has fallen under the spell of Georgia O'Keeffe, and for the first time in her life expects to come to herself, recover herself, make a new life in this place. She has talent, is taking lessons in oils, lives on a ranch, rides daily, and is becoming brown and strong. She is considering having an affair with a cowboy.

(g) A Catholic priest, assigned to the adobe church in the pueblo, an aging Hispanic–Irishman who watches the dance with an indifference amounting to boredom. He is thinking about his added chores for tomorrow—a Monday and therefore ordinarily a holiday, but this year a Holy Day, the Feast of the Assumption, entailing three masses, homilies, and confessions—and about his bad back and his broken radio, an old Philco console. Tonight, unless the repairman shows up, he won't be able to listen to *Lux Radio Theater.*

(h) A radio repairman from Santa Fe, looking for the priest in the crowd. He has fixed the radio. The pueblo, the Corn Dance, the spectacle are old stories to him. All he wants is to find the priest, deliver the Philco, get paid, and get home in time for a cold beer or two before supper.

(i) A technician from the metallurgy lab at Los Alamos, a pale, plump, mustachioed, youngish man, native of Camden, New Jersey, employed by the Manhattan Project but also by an attaché in the Soviet Embassy in Washington. Only son of not impoverished but nonetheless dreary middle-class parents living in the dreariest double-house on the dreariest street in Camden. For him, revelation broke like sunlight through the Jersey winter when he discovered Marx and read him sitting there in a public library like Marx himself, constipated and alone and exhilarated among strangers as the light broke around him. All at once, he saw how it all worked, saw the very mechanism of his sadness and therefore the means of rising above it. Above it he was and above all this, the people whom now he understood, the Indians, the tourists, even the scientist whom he knew by reputation. They, not he, were puppets worked by strings they could not see. But he knew, could see the strings and, best of all, work them himself—for the good of the Soviet Union and therefore for world peace.

(*j*) A tourist from Moline, Illinois, who is too busy taking pictures with his excellent Leica even to take a look for himself, whose concern is only with lighting, focus, composition; who is already casting ahead in his mind to the slide show he'll give at Rotary, and then perhaps he'll take time to take a look at what he recorded—or will he watch the faces of the viewers to gauge his worth from their approval, the way a joke-teller watches the face of the joke-hearer? Yet by no means is he a discontented or unworthy man, being a good husband and father, operating, as he does, a successful chain of dry cleaners in northwest Illinois and even in Davenport, enjoying not only his family but his bowling team and his Masonic lodge. He is an American Legionnaire, a decorated veteran of World War I, holder of the Distinguished Service Cross, an authentic hero who risked his life to save a comrade and who has thought not much about it since.

(CHECK ONE)

Thought Experiment: Draw up an existential-semiotic self-profile or diagram indicating the self's relation to its world (transcending? immanent? intact self among other selves?), identity of self (success or failure of self to perceive itself as a self), self's relation to other selves (world community? elite community? loss of community?), movement of self vis-à-vis world (types of orbit, difficulties of reentry), placement of self in world as evidenced by mood and utterance.

Thus, each character can be plotted, so to speak, on a system of self-coordinates and a rough-and-ready profile of the self arrived at. Such a profile might be called an "existential semiotic graph" of the self. By means of such graphs, selves can be readily compared and contrasted in their salient features—and one's own self more easily identified.

For example, four characters from the Taos Ten:

(1) The nuclear physicist

Self's Relation to World: Transcending.

Self's Relation to Other Selves: A restricted community of a transcending elite (scientific, political, philosophical, musical); also a modified transcendent-immanent sexual Jove-Europa community such as his relationship with blond grad student. E.g., she may not be quite fit to discuss the Bhagavad-Gita with or Planck's equations with, but eminently fit to sleep with.

Identity of Self: A high degree of correspondence between self's habitual mode of existence as transcending self and actual here-and-now life, e.g., scientific project at secret mountain installation, small elite community set down in an immanent world—pueblo, Indians, Corn Dance, tourists, priests—of which he is the onlooker.

Motion of Self vis-à-vis World: Traveling, orbiting, wandering; for a transcending self, one place is as good as any other place to the degree that it provides the immanent raw materials (climate, plutonium, Indians, girls, indigenous culture— Pueblo or Roman Catholic) by means of which the self can both arrive at scientific principles and satisfy its own immanent needs.

Placement (Mood) of Self: Overtly apocalyptic, covertly exultant. Covert exultation accruing from temporary appropriation of godhead by transcending self, e.g., "I am Shiva, Destroyer of Worlds," "We have known sin," etc.

(2) The radio repairman

Self's Relation to World: Immanent, with intact elements.

Self's Relation to Other Selves: Concentric social communities—family, business, social, marketplace, church (Presbyterian), politics (Republican), American.

Identity of Self: Unreflective, consumer-oriented, partly specified by being against *them* (Hispanics, Indians, Catholics), but also against *those*, the transcenders (scientists, Communists, professors, liberals); yet also to a degree specified as intact self by religious transcendence, i.e., he would say if asked that he believed in God, that he was not God but a son and creature of God, that other men were also sons and therefore his brothers.

Motion of Self vis-à-vis World: Placed in a place, once Texas, now Santa Fe, New Mexico, but not placed like the old Pueblo Indian at the center and navel of the Cosmos. Mood of placement: often aggrieved and frustrated, but also exhibiting a core geniality, reliability, and goodwill: "How you doin', son? Well, all right. You lookin' good. Let me give you a hand with that." Etc.

(3) The divorcée from Westchester

Self's Relation to World: Problematical, with elements of transcendence and immanence. She has left what she conceives as an immanent world of a failed marriage and the boredom of housewifery and is seeking a new world with some vaguely transcending components such as "art."

Self's Relation to Other Selves: Loss of old community; isolated, but with prospects of new community. She envisions both immanent and transcendent relationships, sexual adventures perhaps, but, more important, a meeting of minds with a certain person on such things as reading, ideas, and a co-savoring of local immanent features, e.g., the Corn Dance. Further, she has begun an expensive collection of primitive kachina dolls and regularly visits all festivals at the pueblos. She has also registered for a course in flamenco guitar.

Identity of Self: Tentative and problematic. Her own perception of herself is subject to others' perception of her. For example, at this very moment at the Corn Dance she is aware that the scientist and his friend have noticed her, and so she is acutely conscious of not appearing to them either as tourist or as local dried-up leather-skinned dykeish Anglo. So she's dressed casually in jeans (long before the current craze) and Eastern blouse. Her silver-and-turquoise jewelry is old, heavy, and oxidized and not the new tourist junk. Even her mien, her way of looking at the dancers, is both casual and calculated: I've seen this before, true, and some of

it is hokey and put on for the tourists, but still
it's a fascinating spectacle, isn't it?

Movement of Self vis-à-vis the World: Exilic. She's
left her old home for good, glad to do it, and
newly arrived at her new home, where she'll
stay. She's begun her new life but has not
yet quite achieved total reentry into her new
world.

(4) The Catholic priest

Self's Relation to World: Specified by relation to
God, i.e., self, world, and other selves seen as
created by God; selves in the world yet capable
of transcending world through love of other
selves and of God. Yet this relation has for him
grown perfunctory and quotidian over the
years, giving ground to loneliness, dislike and
fear of bishop, and consumership, e.g., *Lux
Radio Theater*, Brooklyn Dodgers, a nip or
two or three of Bushmills before supper. An
humble and mediocre man, he is actually a
better priest than he knows, a soft touch for
beggars and drunks, and dutiful in the discharge
of his priestly obligation.

Self's Relation to Other Selves: Good-natured and
dutiful, with tendencies to accept both the
deferences accorded his social role as priest and
the ambiguities of his priesthood as perceived
by the Indians who accept him—and the
kachinas of the West—with varying admix-
tures of indifference, belief, and unbelief.

Identity of Self: Intact and secure in its relation to God, yet hardly afire with love of God and fellow man. Secure also in his identity as a member of a special class of selves, i.e., the priesthood, with its promised reward in heaven, yet aware too of his failings and accordingly staking a great deal on the mercy of God. Differs from transcending community of scientists and artists in his recognition of his own creatureliness and limitations. His major semiotic self-deception is his acquiescence in the *sign* and role with which the world invests him, that of a priest with attendant mien and costume rather than the *signified*, a man who has a vocation and acts accordingly.

Movement of Self vis-à-vis World: Ambiguously at home; that is to say, he is at home in his homelessness in that he would assent to the proposition that, like all men, he is a pilgrim and wayfarer not at home in this world and bound for his true home elsewhere; but he is also at home in the worldly sense of being at home, e.g., like the radio repairman, he enjoys the comfort of his rectory, his good Indian cook, the companionship of two good friends, three Bushmills before supper, and above all the prospect of a Dodger–Yankee World Series. Though he accepts his identity as pilgrim, wayfarer, priest, and servant of God, he dreads the likelihood of being assigned to the Hopi reservation, the true boondocks.

Now, imagine that you yourself are present at the Taos Corn Dance, where the old gods are still remembered, plus the new God, plus the competing spirits of transcendence of the modern age—something new in the Cosmos—plus the acceptance of the demotion to the pure spirit of immanence —also something new.

Chart your own semiotic profile.

(14) THE ORBITING SELF: *Reentry Problems of the Transcending Self, or Why it is that Artists and Writers, Some Technologists, and indeed Most People have so much Trouble Living in the Ordinary World*

In the age of science, scientists are the princes of the age. Artists are not. So that even though both scientists and artists achieve transcendence over the ordinary world in their science and art, only the scientist is sustained in his transcendence by the exaltation of the triumphant spirit of science and by the community of scientists.

It is perhaps no accident that at the high tide of physics in the nineteenth and early twentieth centuries, the great revolutionary physicists—e.g., Faraday, Maxwell, Bohr, Einstein—were also men of remarkable integrity and exultant wholeness of character, of generosity and benignity. Compare the lives and characters of the comparably great in literature at the same time: Dostoevsky, Baudelaire, Kafka, Joyce, Lawrence, Hemingway.

With the disappearance of the old cosmological myths and the decline of Judaeo-Christianity and the rise of the autonomous self, science and art, one the study of secondary causes, the other the ornamental handmaiden of rite and religion, were seized upon and elevated to royal highroads of transcendence in their own right. Such transcendence was available not only to the scientists and artists themselves but to a community of fellow scientists and students, and to the readers and listeners and viewers to whom the "statements" of art, music, and literature were addressed.

But what is not generally recognized is that the successful launch of self into the orbit of transcendence is necessarily attended by problems of reentry. What goes up must come down. The best film of the year ends at nine o'clock. What to do at ten? What did Faulkner do after writing the last sentence of *Light in August*? Get drunk for a week. What did Dostoevsky do after finishing *The Idiot*? Spend three days and nights at the roulette table. What does the reader do after finishing either book? How long does his exaltation last?

The only exception to this psychic law of gravity seems to be not merely the great physicists at the high tide of modern physics but any scientist absorbed in his science when the exaltation of science sustains one in a more or less permanent orbit of transcendence—or perhaps the rare Schubert who even during meals wrote lieder on the tablecloth or the Picasso in a restaurant who instead of eating bread molded it into statuettes.

But the most spectacular problems of reentry seem to be experienced by artists and writers. They, especially the latter, seem subject more than most people to estrangement from the society around them, to neurosis, psychosis, alcoholism, drug addiction, epilepsy, florid sexual behavior, solitariness, depression, violence, and suicide.

Question: Is this the case because

(*a*) Genius is close to madness (Plato)?

(*b*) Modern society, especially American, is crass, materialistic, money-grubbing, and status-seeking, a nation of Yahoos and Babbitts, and the artist who is in pursuit of truth and beauty is entitled to be alienated (Gauguin, Flaubert, Lewis, et al.)?

(*c*) Art is an expression of sublimated libidinal energies (Freud)? Since the artist is presumably either oversupplied with such energies or overly repressed, it is only to be expected that he or she might also be subject to the various maladies attendant upon repressed sexuality.

(*d*) Art, unlike science, is a kind of play (Dewey)? Therefore, artists are expected to behave like children.

(*e*) Both art and science are ways of knowing and as such are the greatest pleasures of which man is capable (Aristotle, Aquinas)? So great, in fact, that the ordinary pursuits of life are spoiled by contrast and so the artist must go to heroic lengths to render life tolerable outside his art. What Einstein said of science might be said of art: I went into science to escape the intolerable dreariness of everyday life.

(CHECK ONE)

Art, like science, entails a certain abstraction from its subject matter, albeit a different order of abstraction. And the better the artist, the greater the distance of abstraction. Thus, writers like Sidney Sheldon and Harold Robbins are as much in the marketplace as any other producer or seller. But writers like Joyce, Faulkner, Proust are able to write about the marketplace and society only in the degree that they distance themselves from it—whether by exile, alcohol, or withdrawal to a cork-lined room.

Like scientists, artists make general statements about the world, not about forms of energy exchange but what it is like to live in the world—statements which reader or viewer confirms by his assent and pleasure (where else does the reader's pleasure come from but the reader's recognition of and identification with the artist's work?), just as the scientist confirms scientific statements by tests and reading pointers.

Although science and art are generally taken to be not merely different but even polar opposites—the one logical, left-brained, unemotional, Apollonian, analytical, discursive, abstract; the other intuitive, playful, concrete, Dionysian, emotional—the fact is that both are practiced at a level of abstraction, both entail transactions with symbols and statements about the world, both are subject to confirmation or disconfirmation. The pleasure of reading Dostoevsky derives from a recognition and a confirmation. The dismay of looking at a bad painting or reading a bad poem is a disconfirmation.

For a writer to reenter the world he has written about is no small feat. At the least, it is a peculiar exercise, even uncanny—like Kierkegaard going out into the street every hour during work and blinking at the shopkeepers. At the worst, it proves impossible, issuing in the familiar catastrophes to which writers fall prey.

Thought Experiment: A deductive-empirical exercise, something like Mendeleev's project of deducing the periodic table of the elements, then looking around to see if there are actual elements which fit in the table.

This enjoyable exercise is the deduction of the various possible reentry modes of the artist-writer or reader-viewer from the semiotic options theoretically available to any person so abstracted from the world.

The experiment: Start with the *world*, that is, the same somewhat deranged place which everyone experiences in more or less the same degree. The *world* is the aggregate of your perceived environment encoded by signs: other people, family, house, marketplace, culture, myth, TV, past, future, and God as more or less real depending on whether you are an unbeliever or a believer, and even if the latter, then God as more or less problematical.

Next, there is the self, the individual conscious artist-writer reader-viewer self, the movable piece in the world, like a token in a Monopoly game.

The problem for the movable piece: How do you go about living in the world when you are not working at your art, yet still find yourself having to get through a Wednesday afternoon?

Note: This game can be played by artists and writers or by non-artists and non-writers, in fact by all true denizens of the age, that is, any person in the culture who feels himself orbiting the world, out of the here-and-now, out of life in a place and a time, and experiencing difficulty with reentry into such a life.

In order to understand the purpose of the exercise and be instructed by it, let us make the following assumptions which are probably more true than false but which at any rate I will not take the trouble to defend: that the present world is in some sense deranged, the center is not holding, that the plight of the self of the artist-writer is at least in part a historical phenomenon and not an essential property of being an artist-writer; that there may have been other times and other places, whether one wishes to call them an age of faith or an age of myth, in which men perceived a saving relationship to God, the Cosmos, the world, and each other. In such times the self did not feel displaced, or if it did, it understood its displacement. The artist-writer did not, presumably, feel the same compulsion to assert his individual genius-self as would the artist today. It did not, presumably, occur to the Chartres sculptor to sign his name on the toe of an apostle he had finished on the West Portal. (Or to the Lascaux Cave painter.) Though he was a sinful man like other men and subject to certain whims and antics, he would not, presumably, have understood the nineteenth-century English poet who utters a cry: "O world! O life! O time!" and sails out in the Bay of Naples to a suicide by drowning. Or the twentieth-century American novelist riding trains through the haunted towns of America and writing: "O lost, and by the wind grieved, ghost, come back again."

Options of reentry into such a world are: (1) reentry uneventful and intact, (2) reentry accomplished through anesthesia, (3) reentry accomplished by travel (geographical), (4) reentry accomplished by travel (sexual), (5) reentry by return, (6) reentry by disguise, (7) reentry by Eastern window, (8) reentry refused, exitus into deep space (suicide), (9) reentry deferred, (10) reentry by sponsorship, (11) reentry by assault.

Object of experiment: to discover (1) which option you prefer and (2) which option is in fact open to you.

Explanation of Options:

(1) Successful and uneventful reentry, self intact. Theoretically, it is possible for the abstracted self to reenter the world as easily as a doctor leaving his office for Wednesday afternoon golf or the Chartres sculptor going home to sup with his family.

Was this not in fact the case with William Faulkner, doing a morning's work, then strolling in the town square to talk to the farmers and have a Coke at Reed's drugstore? Not quite. Though Faulkner went to lengths to pass himself off as a farmer among farmers, farmer he was not. A charade was being played.

Was it not the case with Sören Kierkegaard, who, every hour, would jump up from his desk, rush out into the streets of Copenhagen, and pass the time with shopkeepers? No, because, by his own admission, he was playing the game of being taken for an idler at the very time he was writing ten books a year.

Only one example comes to mind of a writer who, though performing at a very high level of twentieth-century art, nevertheless manages to live on one of the few remaining islands of a more or less intact culture, in the very house where she was born, to enter into an intercourse with the society around her as naturally as the Chartres sculptor, to appear as herself, her self, the same self, both to fellow writer and to fellow townsman: Eudora Welty. Perhaps also William Carlos Williams.

If you do not think this remarkable, imagine that you have lived your entire life in the house where you were born. For an American, an uncanny, even an unsettling fantasy.

(2) Reentry accomplished through anesthesia. One can simply render the intolerable tolerable by a chemical assault on the cortex of the brain, generally by alcohol, and generally by writers. It has been observed that artists live longer and drink less than writers. Perhaps they are rescued from the ghostliness of self by the things and the doings of their art. The painter and the sculptor are the Catholics of art, the writer is the Protestant. The former have the sacramentals, the concrete intermediaries between themselves and creation —the paint, the brushes, the fruit, the bowl, the table, the model, the mountain, the handling and muscling of clay. The writer is the Protestant. He works alone in a room as bare as a Quaker meeting house with nothing between him and his art but a Scripto pencil, like God's finger touching Adam. It is harder on the nerves.

WHY WRITERS DRINK

He is marooned in his cortex. Therefore it is his cortex he must assault. Worse, actually. He, his self, is marooned in his left cortex, locus of consciousness according to Eccles. Yet his work, if he is any good, comes from listening to his right brain, locus of the unconscious knowledge of the fit and form of things. So, unlike the artist who can fool and cajole his right brain and get it going by messing in paints and clay and stone, the natural playground of the dreaming child self, there sits the poor writer, rigid as a stick, pencil poised, with no choice but to wait in fear and trembling until the spark jumps the commissure. Hence his notorious penchant for superstition* and small obsessive and compulsive acts such as lining up paper exactly foursquare with desk. Then, failing in these frantic invocations and after the right brain falls as silent as the sphinx—what else can it do?—nothing remains, if the right won't talk, but to assault the left with alcohol, which of course is a depressant and which does of course knock out that grim angel guarding the gate of Paradise and let the poor half-brained writer in and a good deal else besides. But by now the writer is drunk, his presiding left-brained craftsman-consciousness laid out flat, trampled by the rampant imagery from the right and a horde of reptilian demons from below.

(3) Reentry accomplished by travel (geographical). The self leaves home because home has been evacuated, not bombed out, but emptied out by the self itself. That is, home, family, neighborhood, and town have been engulfed by the vacuole of self, ingested and rendered excreta. What writer can stay in Oak Park, Illinois? One leaves for another place, but soon it too is ingested and digested. One keeps moving: from Illinois to Minnesota to Paris to Italy to Paris to Spain to Paris to Africa to Paris to Key West to Cuba to Idaho. From Nottinghamshire to Australia to Mexico to Taos to Italy. If one can keep moving and if the places retain sufficient form and decor, the places may not run out before one's life runs out. Hemingway ran out of places. Lawrence did not.

An extreme case of a frantic and failed attempt to enter a habitable world, only to consume it and move on, is Kerouac

---

* Graham Greene, albeit a Christian, was observed by Evelyn Waugh to perform a curious rite before he could get to work. He went out to the street and watched the stream of traffic. When asked what he was doing, he replied that he was waiting for a particular combination of numbers to turn up on a license plate—777. When it did, he went cheerfully to his writing desk.

in *On the Road*. In the course of one book he careens back and forth between New York and California six times—with one Mexican detour.

The road is better than the inn, Cervantes said. True, but he did not reckon with ghostly travelers like the Flying Dutchman.

Note, however, that reentry by travel and also exile (see below) nearly always takes place in a motion from a northern place to a southern place, generally a Mediterranean or Hispanic-American place, from a Protestant or post-Protestant place stripped by religion of sacrament and stripped by the self of all else, to a Catholic or Catholic-pagan place, a culture exotic but not too exotic (Bali wouldn't work), vividly informed by rite, fiesta, ceremony, quaint custom, manners, and the like. This is by no means a Counter-Reformation victory because the attraction is not the Catholic faith—which is absolutely the last thing the autonomous self wants—but the decor and artifact of Catholic belief: the Pamplona festival, the Taxco cathedral, Mardi Gras, and such.

The attraction between the noughted self and the fiesta (quite literally a feast for the starved vacuole of self) exists on a continuum of affinities: at one end, say, the serious yet finally hopeless nostalgia of Henry Adams at Mont-Saint-Michel, at the other the more commonplace delectation of, say, Oppenheimer and Lawrence at a Pueblo festival in New Mexico which, with its outlandish admixture of Catholic and pagan rites, allows the self the best, it thinks, of both worlds: to keep its distance and at the same time savor the esthetic of the spectacle.*

---

* It is a nice ambiguity that Catholics have the least use for the very thing, if not the only thing, for which they are admired, the artifacts, the accidentals, of Catholicism, e.g., the buildings, folkways, music, and so on. Thus, a trivial by-product of New Orleans Catholicism, Mardi Gras, has been seized on by tourists, appropriated by local Protestants, promoted by the Chamber of Commerce, as the major cultural attraction. Nice am-

(4) Reentry by travel (sexual). One has a succession of
lovers of the opposite sex, the same sex, or both. It is difficult
to imagine the self of the autonomous artist in his singular and
godlike abstraction from the ordinary world of men settling
down with a wife and family any more than Jove settling
down with Juno. Juno—yuck! Wife, children, home, fireside,
TV, patio, Medicare in Florida, growing old together, John
Anderson, my jo, John—yuck! Better to grow old alone in
the desert, sit on a rock like a Navajo. But how lovely are the
daughters of men! Indeed, heterosexual intercourse is the very
paradigm of the reentry of the ghost-self back into the in-
carnate world whence it came. Not *cogito ergo sum*—God,
how sick is the self of three hundred years of that cogitation,
a very bad French connection—but rather: If I enter you, I
am alive, even human.

Further exercises: Why are so many artist-writers homosexual? Because the estrangement of the self can be so extreme
that not even the welcoming woman can be used as a portal
of reentry—on the contrary, she becomes the voracious

biguity, I say, because each party is content to have it so. Nobody is
offended.

The Catholic is content to practice his faith in a dumpy church in York,
while the tourists gape at the great nacreous pile of the York minster, an
artifact of a former Catholic culture, as beautiful as the shell of a cham-
bered nautilus and as empty. It is not argumentative, I think, to note the
niceness of the ambiguity because, if the Catholic is content to have it so,
so is the unbeliever. Thus, the esthetic delight of, say, Hemingway in the
Catholic decor of Pamplona would perhaps be matched by his contempt
for actual Catholic practice in Oak Park, Illinois. It is an ambiguity because it can be given two equally plausible interpretations, Catholic and
non-Catholic. The Catholic: what matters to me is faith and practice; the
cathedrals and fiestas are incidental. The non-Catholic: what is attractive
to me is the Catholic decor, cathedrals, and fiestas; what I want no part
of is the belief and practice, which is often in bad taste, if not vulgar.
Both are right. Catholic practice is often drab or outlandish, drab in Oak
Park, Illinois, outlandish in Chichicastanango. And yet the beautiful York
minster is empty. It is a nice ambiguity because each party is content that
the other have it his own way.

vagina, the pure negativity which, risking nothing, maliciously requires performance and therefore threatens to expose one's noughtness. If so, better to cast one's lot with one's own kind, own sex.

And why are artist-writers more promiscuous than scientists? Because science works better, this is the age of science, scientists are the princes of the age, while artist-writers are the frantic Lazaruses at the feast, hungering for crumbs like the dogs, the while scratching and screwing around under the table.

(5) Reentry by return. The options of travel and exile may be exhausted, yet instead of despairing, the traveler may hit upon one last alternative: the return. Why not go back to the very place one left, as a kind of deliberate exercise of freedom? Not only is it not the case that you can't go home again, you may have to—back to the evacuated, bombed-out homeplace, a ruin which by the very fact of its abandonment has in the long interval of one's absence magically acquired a certain solidity and integrity of its own. The Southern writer who put Valdosta behind him as fast and far as Doc Holliday and roamed the world from Martha's Vineyard to Cuernavaca now at last gets a hankering for home. And goes home—for a while. It's one thing to develop a nostalgia for home while you're boozing with Yankee writers in Martha's Vineyard or being chased by the bulls in Pamplona. It's something else to go home and visit with the folks in Reed's drugstore on the square and actually listen to them. The reason you can't go home again is not because the down-home folks are mad at you—they're not, don't flatter yourself, they couldn't care less—but because once you're in orbit and you return to Reed's drugstore on the square, you can stand no more than fifteen minutes of the conversation before you head for the woods, head for the liquor store, or head back to Martha's

Vineyard, where at least you can put a tolerable and saving distance between you and home. Home may be where the heart is but it's no place to spend Wednesday afternoon.

(6) Reentry by disguise. The writer-artist cloaks his noughted self not by wrapping himself in bandages like H. G. Wells's invisible man but by donning the persona-plus-costume worn by those persons who strike him as having most successfully entered the world—or never left it. A more respectable word for such a disguise is role-playing. A hundred years ago, artists, would-be artists, writer-types on the Left Bank wore workers' smocks and berets. More recently, it is jeans, beards, bandit mustaches, denim jackets, tank tops, longhorn belt buckles, and such. But what to do if the crassest members of the marketplace, car salesman, account executive, go cowboy? That is to say, what to do if one's chosen mode of reentry has been co-opted by those very persons who had driven one into outer space to begin with?

The disguise may be behavioral as well as sartorial. Not celebrated in past times for their pugnacity or womanizing, American writers have turned into real cutups, the Southern subspecies often taking the old-fashioned form of the hell-raising passed-out-drunk-in-the-whorehouse good-ol'-boy, the Northern more political: the cocktail-party nose-to-nose you're-deep-down-a-fascist-son-of-a-bitch confrontation, or throwing a punch at the critic who bad-mouthed you in *Time* —though seldom with much effect—or beating up your wife in the kitchen. Poets from all over feel obliged to become more florid sexually. Straight poets on the lecture circuit exchange a black book listing the best lays at the universities where they read. Other poets (male) are noted for flashing and feeling up male graduate students. No more shy Swinburnes or pale Dante Gabriel Rossettis or closet Housmans.

The main difference between latter-day Southern writers and latter-day Northern writers: both are aware of the necessity to shock the reader out of self-unawareness and into recognition of the advanced derangement of the world, but the Southern writer does it by having a character offend against a decayed but still extant ethos—a twin ethos, the Biblical tradition and the honor code. That is, he *sins*, usually sexually, or commits a gothic atrocity against a backdrop of faded Jeffersonian splendor—and sometimes does both at once, like Temple Drake getting corncobbed by Popeye at the old Frenchman place in Faulkner's *Sanctuary*. The latter-day Northern writer, lacking either tradition and having nothing to offend against, must rely on an act of gratuitous and comedic violence—like Michael Milton getting his penis bitten off by Helen Garp in Irving's *The World According to Garp*.

An observation about disguises: The New Orleans French Quarter has long attracted artists and writers and homosexuals for the good and understandable reasons given above: Latinity, quaintness, moderate exoticness, Mardi Gras, the usual para-Catholic aura—and the easiest way to get out of Mississippi and Ohio. But it is also a para-creative aura. Just as the denizens of the Vieux Carré live in the penumbra of the cathedral, they also live in the penumbra of art. Surprisingly little first-class art has come out of the French Quarter, even though it rather self-consciously imitates the decor of the Left Bank, habitat of many great artists years ago. This life style, as it is called, reminds one of the urban cowboy who secretly believes that if he dresses and walks like a cowboy, he may be a cowboy. Faulkner, never one to do things halfway, made extravagant use of standard modes of reentry in New Orleans, not merely geographical and perhaps sexual modes, not merely alcohol, but also a regular repertory of disguises. In the Vieux Carré he made appearances as a wounded veteran with swagger stick and a bogus steel plate in his head, a hard-drinking pre-hippie vagrant Left-Bank type—and wrote *Mosquitoes*,

a not very good novel. It took the ultimate reentry, the return
—he had to go home—to write *The Sound and the Fury.*
Even then, he had to "be" a farmer on the side. Later he made
the grandest Southern reentry of all, as a Virginia horseman.

A prediction: What with artist types and writer types and
homosexuals (who must be applauded for their good taste in
cities: New Orleans, San Francisco, Key West) taking over
such places as the French Quarter, and business types and
lawyer types going cowboy, I predict that working artists and
writers will revert to the vacated places. In fact, they're already turning up in ordinary houses and ordinary streets long
since abandoned by the Hemingways and Agees. Soon they'll
be wearing ordinary shirts and pants and Thom McAn shoes,
not altogether unconsciously, but as a kind of exercise in the
ordinary. What else? Where would you rather be if you were
James Agee now and alive and well: stumbling around
Greenwich Village boozed to the gills, or sitting on the front
porch of a house on a summer evening in Knoxville?

(7) Reentry by Eastern window. Angle of reentry too
shallow, skip back into space, out of singular self in a singular
place back into Cosmic Self, and out of linear time and into
the cycles of reincarnation and the Eternal Return. Comet
orbit.

The self escapes the burden of itself and achieves *satori*
through the negating of self, the *atman*, with the Cosmic Self,
the *Brahman* of Hinduism.

Such a disposal of the self was ever an attractive option,
what with the perennial inability of the self to perceive itself,
but in this age is more attractive than ever as a consequence
of the modern historical predicament of the self. The movement of science tends to abstract the self from the world both
for the scientist and for the layman, who is willy-nilly abstracted by the triumphant spirit of science without, however,
being compensated by the joy of the practice of science. The

movement of art is toward the isolation and sequestering of the artist as individual in pursuit of art.

Hence the openness of the Eastern window, particularly in California, where the options of reentry often make their first appearance.

There are characteristic affinities between the mode of reentry by the Eastern window and certain other modes of reentry, e.g., the travel and exile modes, often with a dash of science for seasoning.

Examples: English writers in Hollywood—Huxley, Isherwood, et al. Reentry by travel (geographical) plus travel (homosexual) plus Eastern window, the multiple reentry mode underwritten by science (mind-altering drugs opening the doors of perception and assisting the self in its escape from itself).

It is no accident that the post-Protestant English in the van of the scientific and industrial revolution for two centuries were also the discoverers and masters of characteristic reentry modes, especially travel (geographical and sexual) and disguises. It is no coincidence that the English are not only the best actors in the world but the best spies. The modern Englishman can become anyone else. The prototypical Englishman of the twentieth century is not John Bull or Colonel Blimp but Lawrence in Arabia, Olivier in *The Entertainer*, Maugham in the Secret Service.

Do you think it is an accident that all the best writers of spy novels are English?

(8) Refusal of reentry and exitus forever into deep space, which is to say, suicide. Suicide, strangely enough, though the direst of options, is often the most honest, in the sense that the suicide may have run out of the other options and found them lacking. Suicide, that is to say, is arguably a more logical option than a constant recycling of past options— from booze to Spain to broads and back, from booze to Spain

and so on; from cruising Buena Vista Park for the five hundredth fellatio.

(9) Reentry deferred: Self on indefinite hold in orbit. That is to say, the withdrawal of the artist. E.g., Salinger in the woods, Proust in the cork-lined room. Thus, there is no a priori semiotic reason, after all, why the self must reenter the world. It can simply maintain the artistic posture throughout the day, at four o'clock in the afternoon, and have no more to do with the world than a Carthusian monk who receives his food through a turnstile.

(10) Reentry under the direct sponsorship of God. It is theoretically possible, if practically extremely difficult, to reenter the world and become an intact self through the reentry mode Kierkegaard described when he noted that "the self can only become itself if it does so transparently before God." This is in fact, according to both Kierkegaard and Pascal, the only viable mode of reentry, the others being snares and delusions.

There are at least two reasons, having to do with the nature of the age, why this option is so difficult.

One is that from the abstracted perspective of the sciences and arts—an attitude of self-effacing objectivity which through the spectacular triumph of science has become the natural stance of the educated man—God, if he is taken to exist at all, is perforce understood as simply another item in the world which one duly observes, takes note of, and stands over against.

The other reason is that the God-party, at least those who say "Lord Lord" most often, are so ignorant and obnoxious that most educated people want no part of them. If they're for it, then I can't go far wrong in being against it.

It is true that both St. Paul and God are on record as preferring simple folk to the overeducated, especially philosophers. But media preachers have little reason to take comfort. Being uneducated is no guarantee against being obnoxious.

Question: Who is the most obnoxious, Protestants, Catholics, or Jews?

Answer: It depends on where you are and who you are talking to—though it is hard to conceive any one of the three consistently outdoing the other two in obnoxiousness. Yet, as obnoxious as are all three, none is as murderous as the autonomous self who, believing in nothing, can fall prey to ideology and kill millions of people—unwanted people, old people, sick people, useless people, unborn people, enemies of the state —and do so reasonably, without passion, even decently, certainly without the least obnoxiousness.

Religion, at any rate, has been having a bad time of it lately, perhaps for good and sufficient reason. By and large, scientists and artists and the autonomous self have gotten rid of God, whether or not for good reason, whether or not with catastrophic consequences, remains to be seen.

In any case, reentry into ordinary life, into concrete place and time, from the strange abstractions of the twentieth century, the reentry undertaken under the direct sponsorship of God, is a difficult if not nigh-impossible task. Yet there have existed, so I have heard, a few writers even in this day and age who have become themselves transparently before God and managed to live intact through difficult lives, e.g., Simone Weil, Martin Buber, Dietrich Bonhoeffer. Some have even outdone Kierkegaard and seen both creation and art as the Chartres sculptor did, as both dense and mysterious, gratuitous, anagogic, and sacramental, e.g., Flannery O'Connor.

(11) Reentry by assault. The writer-artist makes sure that he is in the world and that he is real by taking on the world, usually by political action and, more often than not, revolutionary. Even if one is imprisoned by the state—especially if

one is imprisoned—one can be certain of being human. Ghosts can't be imprisoned. This stratagem is more available to European writers, who are taken more seriously than American writers. The secret envy of American writers: Alexander Solzhenitsyn. Despite their most violent attacks on the state and the establishment, nobody pays much attention to American writers, least of all the state. To have taken on the state and defeated it, like Solzhenitsyn, is beyond the wildest dreams of the American writer. Because the state doesn't care. This indifference leads to ever more frantic attempts to attract attention, like an ignored child, even to the point of depicting President Johnson and Lady Bird plotting the assassination of Kennedy in Barbara Garson's *MacBird!*, or President Nixon having sex with Ethel Rosenberg and being buggered by Uncle Sam in Times Square in Robert Coover's *The Public Burning*.

Still, no one pays attention.

A paradigm of this generally failed reentry option: a lonely "radical" American writer standing outside the White House gate, screaming obscenities about this fascist state, dictatorship, exploitation of minorities, suppression of freedom of speech, and so on and on—all the while being ignored by President, police, and passersby.

There are worse things than the Gulag.

Thought Experiment: The Reentry Quiz

Object: To enable you to calculate your own apogee of transcendence and your corresponding need of reentry.

Method: Score yourself by checking those avenues of reentry which you find peculiarly, even compulsively, attractive.

Reentry by

(1) —— anesthesia (alcohol, pot, cocaine, etc.)

(2) —— travel (geographical, e.g., Appalachian Trail, Greek Islands, etc.)

(3) —— travel (sexual)

(4) —— return (back to Valdosta, back to downtown Philadelphia, etc.)

(5) —— disguise (e.g., Southern male writer as good ol' boy, Northern male writer as Brooklynite turned Connecticut Yankee with L. L. Bean boots)

(6) —— Eastern window (pilgrimage to Katmandu or to Trungpa's commune in Colorado)

(7) —— deep space (suicide)

(8) —— reentry deferred, permanent orbit (Salinger in the woods, Boo Radley holed up in Alabama house for forty years)

(9) —— sponsorship (conversion)

(10) —— assault (murderous political hatreds, fantasies of assassination or taking vicarious pleasure in same)

(CHECK APPROPRIATE OPTIONS. ADD SCORE)

NOTE: A high score measures the apogee of your orbit but is not necessarily bad. Faulkner might have scored a 5 (see reentry options 1, 2, 3, 4, 5), Malcolm Lowry a 6, William Burroughs a 7, and Erle Stanley Gardner, for all I know a 0.

A high score does no more than measure without prejudice the apogee of one's orbit of transcendence with its attendant triumphs and miseries.

(15) THE EXEMPTED SELF: *How Scientists Don't Have to Take Account of Themselves and Other Selves in their Science and Some Difficulties that Arise when they have to*

Why do scientists dislike what is apparently the case, that *Homo sapiens sapiens* appeared very recently and very suddenly, in a few hundred thousand years more or less of the Late Pleistocene, perhaps even less—in a word, in less time, cosmologically speaking, than it takes to tell the Biblical story of creation; that the peculiar characteristics of man, the explosive growth of the cortex and 60 percent increase in brain volume, emergence of language, consciousness, self, art, religion, science, occurred in cosmic time in the wink of an eye; that though it is Darwin, not Wallace, who gets the credit for the theory of evolution, it was Wallace, not Darwin, who seems to be right in saying that all men, even the most primitive, come fully equipped with the same neocortex and that all men have made the same unprecedented crossover into language and culture; that the brain of the most "primitive" man is not discernibly different from the brain of Beethoven and therefore cannot be accounted for by Darwin's theory of the gradual adaptation of a species to its environment by the natural selection of those traits which best equip it for survival?

Two dogmas:

One, neo-Darwinian theory: Man arose through the chance encounter of molecules and the survival of those aggregations of molecules, i.e., organisms which through the random accumulation of small mutations are best equipped to live in changing environments. If Darwin was right, asked Wallace, why does the Tierra del Fuegan possess a brain not discernibly different from, say, Einstein's or Beethoven's, which he does not need?

Two, so-called scientific creationism: The origin of the species did not occur through evolution over millions of years but through separate acts of God.

Both appear to be unlikely.

Darwin was right about the fact of evolution, and his contribution was unprecedented. Evolution is not a theory but a fact. For a fact, the dinosaurs were here 75 million years ago and were supplanted by mammals. For a fact, man arose from more primitive hominids.

Current evolutionary theory, however, has trouble accounting for the facts of evolution. So unsatisfactory is neo-Darwinism that some scientists have gone far afield for explanations. Francis Crick, co-winner of the Nobel Prize for the discovery of the structure of DNA, believes that DNA could only have arrived from space, sent in the form of bacteria from more advanced civilizations. Sir Fred Hoyle suggests the bacteria might have arrived through encounters with the tails of comets. As fanciful as such notions are, they seem to these scientists less inadequate than the current evolutionary theory.

Difficulties arise when triadic creatures (scientists) try to explain evolution through exclusively dyadic events. Neo-Darwinian theory has trouble accounting for the strange, sudden, and belated appearance of man, the conscious self which speaks, lies, deceives itself, and also tells the truth. It gives an admirable account of the variations in the beaks of Galapagos finches, but what does it have to say about Darwin himself, sitting by his fireside in Kent and hitting on a theory which assigns all of life into a sphere of interaction and immanence while covertly elevating himself into the sphere of transcendence, and worrying about whether he or Wallace was going to publish first?

The current heated controversy between evolutionists and "scientific creationists" is one of the most peculiar in the history of science, peculiar in the way in which dogma is concealed and smuggled in by both sides.

Scientific creationist: there is scientific evidence of a historical deluge, the Biblical flood, of the separateness of the species, and little or no evidence of intermediate forms. (Concealed dogma: as a fundamentalist Christian, I believe literally in the Genesis account of creation and require that scientific theory be harmonized accordingly.)

Neo-Darwinian: the overwhelming evidence is that evolution occurred through the natural selection of those organisms which through the random accumulation of small mutations are best adapted to a changed environment. (Concealed dogma: I, the scientist, a triadic creature possessed of a transcending objective consciousness and a desire to write papers which will be confirmed or disconfirmed by my colleagues, also require that my data conform to the dyadic principles of interaction which obtain in physics, chemistry, and the biology of lower organisms.)

As unsatisfactory as the battle lines, as presently drawn, may be, one must nevertheless throw in with the modern evolutionist, if only for the reason that his position, if wrong, is in the end self-correcting, whereas that of the scientific creationist is not.

The battle is, in fact, a marvelous waste of energy.

The Christians need not have got in such a sweat. The evolutionary facts about the emergence of man, e.g., the sudden appearance of *Homo sapiens sapiens* (Cro-Magnon man) no more than 35 thousand years ago, are as spectacular as the account in Genesis and allow hardly less room for theology.

Scientists should be less worried about overt intrusions by religion upon science, which never succeed, and more worried about covert scientific dogma, e.g., that we triadic scientists require that only dyadic events be admissible to scientific theory. For example, scientists have never seriously addressed themselves to the phenomenon of language, *considered as a natural phenomenon and not as a formal structure*, that salient triadic property of man. It is only when science is willing to focus on what Sebeok calls "the intersection of nature and culture" that the full import of man's emergence in the evolutionary scheme can be calculated.

Question: Why does it make scientists uneasy that it appears to be the case that *Homo sapiens sapiens*, a conscious languaged creature, appeared suddenly and lately—when scientists profess to be interested in what is the case, that is, the evidence?

(*a*) Because scientists are understandably repelled by the theory of the special creation of man by God, in Biblical time, say 6004 B.C. at 11 a.m. on a Wednesday morning.

(*b*) Because scientists find it natural to deal with matter in interaction and with energy exchanges and don't know what to make of such things as consciousness, self, and symbols and even sometimes deny that there are such things, even though they, the scientists, act for all the world as if they were conscious selves and spend their lives transacting with symbols.

(*c*) Because scientists are uneasy with discontinuities, even when there is evidence of such discontinuity in the appearance of man in all his contrarieties. Revealed religion has its dogmas, e.g., thou shalt not kill. But so does science: thou shalt not tolerate discontinuities. The question is which is the more entitled.

(d) Because scientists in the practice of the scientific method, a non-radical knowledge of matter in interaction, often are not content with the non-radicalness of the scientific method and hence find themselves located in a posture of covert transcendence of their data, which is by the same motion assigned to the sphere of immanence. Hence, scientists operate in the very sphere of transcendence which is not provided for in their science. Given such a posture, it is not merely an offense if a discontinuity turns up in the sphere of immanence, the data, but especially if the discontinuity seems to allow for the intervention of God. A god is already present. A scientist is a god to his data. And if there is anything more offensive to him than the suggestion of the existence of God, it is the existence of two gods.

(CHECK ONE)

How can an immanent theory of evolution mounted from the transcending posture of science account for the appearance in the Cosmos of a triumphant, godlike, murderous alien, the only alien in the Cosmos, *Homo sapiens sapiens*, e.g., the scientist himself?

Which is to say only that Darwin was a very great scientist, that Wallace was a little nutty, sometimes obnoxiously occult, but in the end may have been closer to the truth about man.

Thought Experiment: You are a high-school student. In school, you attend biology class where you are taught modern evolutionary theory. On Sunday, you go to church, where you hear the story of creation from a fundamentalist preacher. Then you go to college and hear a liberal professor-theologian who teaches a class on Science and the World's Great Religions. You speak to the professor-theologian about the dispute between the preacher and the biology teacher. The professor-theologian smiles and says: Both are right.

Genesis is a mythical account of the origin of the Cosmos, the origin of life and the origin of man. There is a certain truth in this myth. There are other cosmological myths, each valid in its own way. There is such a thing as mythical truth. Indeed, the neo-Darwinian theory of evolution through mutations and natural selection is in fact more impressive evidence of God's majesty than the notion that God created the millions of species by separate and arbitrary acts of creation like a child modeling a menagerie out of clay.

The student says: None of you is satisfactory. All of you are unconvincing—and you, the professor-theologian, may be the worst of the lot, satisfying nobody and papering over everything in the name of nothing. How can a myth which you say is untrue in the scientific sense be true in another sense? What is the truth? What I want to know is this, and it doesn't seem to be too much to ask: whatever the time and place of the appearance of man, whether it was the Late Pleistocene, the Upper Paleolithic, whether in the caves of the Dordogne or the Neander River—please tell me, leaving God aside, apart from Darwin and Wallace, please tell me, not in detail, but only in the most general and schematic way— please tell me how it came to pass that matter in interaction, a sequence of energy exchanges, neurones firing other neurones like a binary computer, can result in my being conscious, having a self, being able to utter sentences which are more or less true and which you can understand. Please excuse my stupidity, but would someone draw me a picture? Or just tell me *in principle* how this could happen. Or, if there is a soul, please tell me what evidence there is that it exists, and if it does, how it is connected with this compact mass of billions of neurones which is my brain.

How do you think his three elders, the scientist, the preacher, the professor-theologian, each of whom claims knowledge of a certain species of truth, would answer him?

How would you answer him?

(*a*) Stick with current scientific theory. It is more reliable than religion. Indeed, there may not be any such thing as soul, self, consciousness, and the rest.

(*b*) God comes first, above all else, therefore above science. Believe in the Bible, and all else follows.

(*c*) I don't know the answer. Why don't you stop complaining and become an anthropologist, a psycholinguist, or a neurobiologist and try to find out for yourself?

(CHECK ONE)

Question (II): The anomaly of objectivism. In view of the proclaimed neutrality of the scientific method toward God and its openness to evidence, how do you account for the objectivist's dislike of God, even when the possibility of God's existence is raised by a scientist with the highest credentials?

The following incident occurred at Harvard University, presumably a citadel of objective knowledge. I quote from an article by Charles Krauthammer (*The New Republic,* July 25, 1981): "Several years ago the great Australian neurobiologist, Sir John Eccles, ended a Harvard lecture on brain organization by admitting that although evolution could account for the brain, it could not, in his view, account for the mind, with its mysterious capacity for consciousness and thought: only something transcendent could account for that. The audience began hissing."

The anomaly lies in the fact that the Harvard audience, presumably endowed with mind, consciousness, and thought, and presumably with more intellectual curiosity than most, might have been expected to welcome the views of a famous neurobiologist on the subject—particularly in view of the failure of academic psychology even to address itself to these matters.

Why did the Harvard audience hiss Sir John Eccles and not, say, Jane Fonda?

(*a*) Because God and religion have a bad name, and deservedly so, what with the excesses of the Moral Majority and the fundamentalist attack on science and, especially, the absurdity of "scientific creationism."

(*b*) Because, while the scientific method may be officially neutral toward God, scientism, an attitude which extrapolates from the objectivity of the scientific method to an all-construing transcending objectivism, cannot be neutral. There is no room in the Cosmos for an absolutely transcending objective mind and an absolutely transcending God.

(CHECK ONE)

(16) THE LONELY SELF: *Why the Autonomous Self feels so Alone in the Cosmos that it will go to any Length to talk to Chimpanzees, Dolphins, and Humpback Whales*

In recent years a tremendous amount of effort and money has been spent by the government and primatologists in the effort to demonstrate that chimpanzees and other apes can learn human language. Chimps were adopted like children and, unlike children, were subjected to years of concentrated lessons in speech. When attempts to teach chimps to speak failed, sign language was substituted. Glowing successes were reported. Some chimps became famous.

Yet the most recent assessments by responsible scientists are that the primatologists have either deluded themselves or at least made exaggerated claims. It now appears that chimps are not using language after all but are, rather, using signs and responses in order to obtain rewards (e.g., bananas). The basic elements of language are missing: symbols, sentences, productivity, cultural transmission. Now even some of the most evangelical primatologists have modified their claims.

In short, it appears that chimps can't talk, with either their voices or their hands. Or, as Sebeok puts it, animals have communication but not language.

Yet the public perception is that chimps, and perhaps dolphins and the humpback whale, have crossed the language barrier. There are speculations about the mathematical and metaphysical knowledge of dolphins. For example, according to a recent newspaper account, the song of a humpback whale has ten times as many phonemes as does human speech.

Question: Why do people in general want to believe that chimps and dolphins and whales can speak, and why do some scientists in particular want so badly to believe that chimps can speak that they will compromise their own science?

(*a*) Because anyone who has invested reputation, a great deal of effort, time, and money in an experiment wants it to succeed.

(*b*) Because the last three hundred years have seen the dethronement of man from what he believed to be his central position in the Cosmos to an insignificant planet (Copernicus, Galileo), from his uniqueness among the species as the only besouled creature and as created by God in His image (Darwin), and even from the sovereignty of his own consciousness (Freud). Only language and other symbolic behavior (art, music) seems to remain as the sole remaining indisputably unique attribute of man. If language can be shown to be within the capability of apes, dolphins, and humpback whales, the dethronement of man will be complete.

(*c*) Because man is a lonely and troubled species, who does not know who he is or what to do with himself, feeling himself somehow different from other creatures, both superior and inferior—superior because, after all, he studies other animals and writes scientific articles about them, and other animals don't study him; inferior because he is not a very good animal, is often stupid, irrational, and self-destructive—and solitary in the Cosmos, like Robinson Crusoe marooned on an island populated by goats. Therefore, he would like to discover his place in the Cosmos, discover a man Friday, or, failing that, at least teach goats to talk. So anxious, in fact, have some people been to communicate with Washoe, the most famous chimp, that in the attempt to make signs for Washoe three psychologists have had their fingers bitten off for their pains. Alas for man: rebuffed again.

(*d*) Because a primatologist is competing with other primatologists and therefore feels alone even among his colleagues. If he could converse with his chimpanzee, he would have the best of both worlds: (*a*) beat other scientists, and (*b*) have someone to talk to.

If man cannot communicate with other creatures, he is alone with himself. Dr. John Lilly, after claiming all manner of mystical and philosophical knowledge for the dolphin and after spending years trying to communicate with dolphins, changed his profession: to the study of the effect of mind-altering drugs on the individual human consciousness. He jumped from a tank of dolphins into the tank of himself.

Thought Experiment: Imagine that you are the scientist who has at last succeeded in puncturing the last of man's inflated claims to uniqueness in the Cosmos. Now man is proved beyond doubt to be an organism among other organisms, a species in continuity with other species, a creature existing in interaction with an immanent Cosmos like all other creatures, like all elements, molecules, gaseous clouds, novas, galaxies.

Now, having placed man as an object of study in the Cosmos in however an insignificant place, how do *you*, the scientist, the self which hit upon this theory, how do you propose to reenter this very Cosmos where you have so firmly placed the species to which you belong? Who are you who has explained the Cosmos and how do you fit into the Cosmos you have explained?

Having proved your hypothesis, what do you do next? (1) Publish a paper in *Science*? (2) Begin to lobby for the Nobel? (3) Worry about three other scientists who are working on the same project? (4) Get drunk? (5) Go home and quarrel with your wife? (6) Take a girlfriend to a motel and watch *Deep Throat* on closed-circuit TV?

If the last is your choice, explain the connection between the triumph of science as a form of transcendence of the world and pornography as one of the few remaining avenues of reentry.

Carl Sagan is right in ridiculing the absurd pseudosciences now so popular. He is admirable in his defense of science as a reliable and self-correcting method of attaining truth.

Yet the fact is that nowadays there is no piece of nonsense that will not be believed by some and no guru or radio preacher, however corrupt, who will not attract a following.

Question: Why are people these days generally indifferent to science and yet willing to believe any absurd claim and any rascal who puts it forward?

(*a*) Because there is a need in humans for myth, for symbols, to construe and order a confusing and hostile environment—just as there is a need for food, water, shelter, and sex—and the abstract truths in science do not provide this myth.

(*b*) Because, as Chesterton said, when man stops believing in God, he will believe in anything at all.

(CHECK ONE)

Sagan is right in saying that despite all the claims of UFO sightings and encounters of a third kind, extraterrestrial creatures, and such, not a single artifact, e.g., a piece of metal, a bit of clothing of a visitor, a piece of tissue, a fingernail, has been recovered.

Yet Sagan has written whole volumes promoting the probability of the existence of intelligent life on the billions of planets orbiting the billions and billions of stars in our galaxy, let alone the billions of other galaxies—this in spite of the fact that there is no evidence that life exists anywhere else in the Cosmos, let alone intelligent life. Of all the billions of electromagnetic waves from the Cosmos received here on earth, not a single one can be attributed to an ETI.

Therefore, one might ask Sagan the same question he put to UFOers: Of all the countless bits of data received from outer space, the observations of astronomers, the millions of units recorded by radio telescopes, why has not a single bit of information been received which could not be attributed to the random noise of the Cosmos?

Question: Why is Carl Sagan so lonely?

(*a*) Sagan is lonely because, as a true devotee of science, a noble and reliable method of attaining knowledge, he feels increasingly isolated in a world in which, as Bronowski has said, there is a failure of nerve and men seem willing to undertake anything other than the rigors of science and believe anything at all: in Velikovsky, von Daniken, even in Mr. and Mrs. Barney Hill, who reported being captured and taken aboard a spacecraft in Vermont.

(*b*) Sagan is lonely because, after great expectations, he has not discovered ETIs in the Cosmos, because chimpanzees don't talk, dolphins don't talk, humpback whales sing only to other humpback whales, and he has heard nothing but random noise from the Cosmos, and because Vikings 1 and 2 failed to discover evidence of even the most rudimentary organic life in the soil of Mars.

(*c*) Sagan is lonely because, once everything in the Cosmos, including man, is reduced to the sphere of immanence, matter in interaction, there is no one left to talk to except other transcending intelligences from other worlds.

Thought Experiment: You are Sagan and you are monitoring the Cornell University radio telescope at Arecibo, Puerto Rico, when, after years of reception of random noise, you receive a signal which can only be interpreted as representing the prime numbers, 1, 2, 3, 5, 7, 11, 13, 17, 19, 23 . . . Communication is established! The source of the transmission must be Alpha Centauri because of the direction and the transmission time: four years. Years pass. A code is agreed upon. But time is running out. You are growing old. What with the difficulties of encoding and decoding and the period of transmission, there is only time for five simple questions. Which questions would you ask, and how would you answer these five questions from Alpha Centauri?

(1) Are you in continuity with other organisms on P-3, S-G2V (third planet = earth, star G2V = our sun)?

(2) If not, what is nature of discontinuity?

(3) Are you in trouble?

(4) If so, specify.

(5) What information do you need? (E.g., what can we do for you?)

(18) THE DEMONIAC SELF: *Why it is the Autonomous Self becomes Possessed by the Spirit of the Erotic and the Secret Love of Violence, and how Unlucky it is that this should have Happened in the Nuclear Age*

Sören Kierkegaard made a very strange statement. He said that Christianity first brought the erotic spirit into the world. In his arcane style, which often seems designed as much to obfuscate as to enlighten the reader, he wrote: "Sensualism, viewed from the standpoint of Spirit, was first posited by Christianity." Which is to say, not that sensuality had not existed in the world before in paganism, perhaps in its most perfect expression in Greece, "but not as a spiritual category." It existed rather as an expression of harmony and unison. "In the Greek consciousness, the sensuous was under the control of the beautiful personality or, more rightly stated, it was not controlled, for it was not an enemy to be subjugated, not a dangerous rebel who should be held in check." But in the Christian era the sensuous-erotic becomes "a qualified spirituality, that is to say, so qualified that the Spirit excludes it; if I imagine this principle concentrated in a single individual, then I have a concept of the sensuous-erotic genius. This is an idea which the Greeks did not have, which Christianity first brought into the world, even if only in an indirect sense."

The highest expression of the sensuous-erotic genius, in Kierkegaard's view, was Mozart's *Don Giovanni*: "Mozart is the greatest of classic composers and *Don Giovanni* deserves the highest place among all classic works of art."

What is arresting here is Kierkegáard's view that the Don is to be understood not merely as a roué, a dirty old man reverted to his animal appetites, a sinner, or even as a good pagan, a Greek hedonist, but rather as "the inspiration of the flesh by the spirit of the flesh."

Nor is the "sensuous-erotic" to be understood in modern biological terms as the sex drive and need-satisfaction, but rather as the sensual "spirit" and therefore, in Kierkegaard's word, as the "demoniac."

It is this "demoniac" spirit of the erotic which is "posited" by Christianity.

Presumably, Kierkegaard would have no difficulty explaining that national characteristic which has astounded so many foreign visitors to this country: that the United States is at once the most Christian of nations (at least in numbers of churchgoers) and at the same time the most eroticized society in all of history.

For our purposes, which is a much more modest and dialectically less sophisticated approach to such matters, there are two things of value in Kierkegaard's notion of the "spirit of the sensuous-erotic," and I acknowledge the debt fully aware that this particular passage from Kierkegaard was written under one of his pseudonyms and in "the esthetic stage of existence" and hence not necessarily approved by Kierkegaard writing in his "religious stage."

One thing of value is his setting aside the "sensuous-erotic" as a category to be examined in its own right, a category which not only is not to be dismissed as simply sinful but which can in fact produce works of the highest genius, in Kierkegaard's term, "the musical-erotic genius" of *Don Giovanni.* Thus, we are dispensed from the necessity of uttering the usual denunciations of the present age, familiar from both Christian and non-Christian sources, and adducing the usual statistics about the rise in teenage pregnancies, pornography, sex in the media, child molestation, rape, and so on. And dispensed as well from the usual rhetoric of the "sexual revolution"—the Don would have made an ideal subject of a *Playboy* interview or *Playgirl* centerfold (Hugh Hefner in fact might be described as a latter-day, rather washed-out Don; if he were set to music, it would not be by Mozart but by Mantovani)—even to the point of blaming all the woes of the Western world on the repression of sexuality by Christianity. Such denunciations and defenses are remarkable chiefly for their sterility. There is something more than a little dreary about the present standoff between the "sexual revolution" and the Christian counterrevolutionaries. It usually comes down to the Reverend Jerry Falwell confronting Bob Guccione, editor of *Penthouse*, on a talk show. Both men do their usual numbers, the viewer takes sides, and that is that.

But Kierkegaard gives us leave to see both, both Jerry Falwell and Bob Guccione, from a different perspective, as if the TV camera had been dollied backstage, from which vantage point we can see both Guccione and Falwell plus the talk-show host plus the studio audience and form some notion of what is going on with all of them.

Even more valuable is Kierkegaard's characterization of "the spirit of the sensuous-erotic" and his use of the quaint word "demoniac."

"Demoniac" implies possession of the soul by an unbenign spirit. Such a notion comports well with our far more modest semiotic description of the self, not necessarily as a soul or spirit, but in minimal terms as that semiotic entity which is unique in its ability to understand the world but not itself. The science of the scientist can understand everything in the Cosmos but the self of the scientist. It, the self, is therefore a "spiritual" entity, if you like, but an entity anyhow subject to its own modes of existence, triumphs, and disasters and, in this age, its own peculiar predicaments. Not the least benefit of semiotics and Kierkegaard is that we are delivered from the debilitating strictures of modern psychology, which has not the means of saying anything at all about the self, let alone spirit.

Both Kierkegaard and modern semiotics give us leave to speak of the self as being informed—"possessed," if you like, at certain historical stages of belief and unbelief. It becomes possible, whether one believes in God or not, soul or not, to agree that in an age in which the self is not informed by cosmological myths, by totemism, by belief in God—whether the God of Christianity, Judaism, or Islam—it must necessarily and by reason of its own semiotic nature be informed by something else.

Kierkegaard wrote of the relationship between Christianity and "the spirit of the erotic." I wonder what he would have made of the influence of the technological revolution on the spirit of the erotic and whether it is a coincidence that this country is not only the most Christian and most eroticized of all societies but also the most technologically transformed and the most violent. Is there a relationship between the "spirit of the erotic," technology, and violence?

At any rate, one may state the fact in Kierkegaardian terms without pretending to solve the riddle of the relationship:

The fact is that, by virtue of its peculiar relationship to the world, to others, and to its own organism, the autonomous self in a modern technological society is possessed. It is possessed by the spirit of the erotic and the secret love of violence.

The peculiar predicament of the present-day self surely came to pass as a consequence of the disappointment of the high expectations of the self as it entered the age of science and technology. Dazzled by the overwhelming credentials of science, the beauty and elegance of the scientific method, the triumph of modern medicine over physical ailments, and the technological transformation of the very world itself, the self finds itself in the end disappointed by the failure of science and technique in those very sectors of life which had been its main source of ordinary satisfaction in past ages.

As John Cheever said, the main emotion of the adult Northeastern American who has had all the advantages of wealth, education, and culture is disappointment.

Work is disappointing. In spite of all the talk about making work more creative and self-fulfilling, most people hate their jobs, and with good reason. Most work in modern technological societies is intolerably dull and repetitive.

Marriage and family life are disappointing. Even among defenders of traditional family values, e.g., Christians and Jews, a certain dreariness must be inferred, if only from the average time of TV viewing. Dreary as TV is, it is evidently not as dreary as Mom talking to Dad or the kids talking to either.

School is disappointing. If science is exciting and art is exhilarating, the schools and universities have achieved the not inconsiderable feat of rendering both dull. As every scientist and poet knows, one discovers both vocations in spite of, not because of school. It takes years to recover from the stupor of being taught Shakespeare in English Lit and Wheatstone's bridge in Physics.

Politics is disappointing. Most young people turn their backs on politics, not because of the lack of excitement of politics as it is practiced, but because of the shallowness, venality, and image-making as these are perceived through the media—one of technology's greatest achievements.

The churches are disappointing, even for most believers. If Christ brings us new life, it is all the more remarkable that the church, the very bearer of this good news, should be among the most dispirited institutions of the age. The alternatives to the institutional churches are even more grossly dis-

appointing, from TV evangelists with their blown-dry hairdos
to California cults led by prosperous gurus ignored in India
but embraced in La Jolla.

Social life is disappointing. The very franticness of attempts to reestablish community and festival, by partying,
by group, by club, by touristy Mardi Gras, is the best evidence of the loss of true community and festival and of the
loneliness of self, stranded as it is as an unspeakable consciousness in a world from which it perceives itself as somehow estranged, stranded even within its own body, with which it
sees no clear connection.

But there remains the one unquestioned benefit of science:
the longer and healthier life made possible by modern medicine, the shorter work-hours made possible by technology,
hence what is perceived as the one certain reward of the
dreary life of home and the marketplace: recreation.

Recreation and good physical health appear to be the only
unambivalent benefits of the technological revolution.

Four modes of recreation might be deduced from the semiotic which follows upon the placement of an autonomous
unspeakable self in its world. The recreational modes of the
autonomous self are understandable in terms of the semiotic
options open to it, that is, those transactions with its world,
itself, and other selves which are specified by its own placement in its world and its perception of itself as unspeakable.

They are:

Travel, the actual movement of the self in its world.

Sports, the disposing of oneself by contest and in team
sports, the creation of a quasi community and territory, and
the consequent identification of self with *us* against *them.*

Media, those transactions in which the self receives signs
from other selves through a medium. Such a category can
include sign-transactions as diverse as reading *War and Peace,*

watching *Dallas* on TV, listening to The Grateful Dead on tape, hearing Dan Rather on the five-thirty news.

Drugs: the alteration of consciousnes or the anesthetizing of the unspeakability of self.

Sex: the cheapest, most readily available and pleasurable mode of intercourse with other selves and the only mode of intercourse by which the self can be certain of its relationship with other selves—by touching and being touched, by giving and receiving pleasure, by penetrating or being penetrated.

Polarities of the "authentic" *vs*. the "inauthentic" are easily discernible in recreational modes. The criteria of authenticity are not necessarily objective but have rather to do with the rules by which the self allows or disallows its own experience.

For example, in travel, the actual movement of the self in the world to escape the expanding nought of the autonomous self at home, different selves will be disappointed or satisfied or delighted according as the trip falls short of, meets, or exceeds the expectation of the self. But the expectation of the self, to be informed in its nothingness—if only I can get out of this old place and into the new right place, I can become a new person—places a heavy burden on travel.

Three people take a bus tour of Mexico.

The bus breaks down and the tourists have to make an unscheduled stop, an old abandoned monastery converted to a questionable hotel by a questionable hotelier, like Ava Gardner in *Night of the Iguana*.

Traveler *A* is unhappy. She paid for certain accommodations and expects them. Things have gone awry. She makes everyone miserable with her complaints.

Traveler *B* is delighted. Having set great store by this trip, he is disappointed by its routineness, by Latinized Holiday Inns, by condo-rimmed beaches, by his boring fellow tourists.

Now the unexpected happens. He feels he has left the beaten path. With satisfaction he surveys his new lodgings, a monk's cell with adobe walls yea thick—he tells his friends later—and a single window overlooking a lush jungle. An adventure. What next?

Traveler C is neither happy nor unhappy. She knows all about standard bus tours of Mexico and she knows all about the unhappiness of Traveler A. But she also knows all about the happiness of Traveler B and the getting-off-the-beaten-path syndrome. In fact, she's even heard of certain tours where "breakdowns" and "wrong turns" by wayward buses are prearranged. There are any number of converted monasteries in Mexico ministering to this new spiritual need. Yet she wants to make the tour, if only to get away and be let alone, and with minimal expectations. In fact, it is the very ordinariness of the tour and the ordinariness of the break-down which she enjoys. She cultivates the routine as such. Rather than watch the picturesque Mexicans, she finds herself watching her fellow tourists watching the picturesque Mexicans. Joan Didion immortalized Traveler C.

Question: Do you identify with one traveler more than with the others? If you do, are there objective grounds for your preference?

(*a*) I might identify with one or another traveler but it is a subjective choice depending on one's own experience—how many Mexican bus tours you've made, your life situation, and so on. One might be looking for adventure, sex, who knows?—or perhaps one has a rotten job and a rotten marriage and so may want nothing more than a mindless hiatus, so that it doesn't matter whether the bus is lost or found or touring Mexico or Ireland. It's too bad that *A* is unhappy, it is nice that *B* is happy, and a matter of indifference that *C* is neither. But what more is there to say?

(*b*) No, an objective judgment of sorts can be made. Traveler *A* is a nerd, your sub-ordinary unreflective American tourist, not to be identified with and certainly not to be preferred. *B* is better off, but not much. *C* knows this, and though she may not be happy and may not have any expectations, she is nevertheless to be preferred to *A* or *B*. For she is at least coming to the end of her rope, the same rope *A* and *B* have hold of, and will at least find out what is at the end. It is better to know than not to know.

(CHECK ONE)

The expectations of the autonomous self, to be informed in its nothingness—if only I can get out of this old place and into the right new place, I can become a new person—pins a quasi-religious hope on, of all things, travel.

It is notable that when travel as a recreational mode is experienced vicariously through the media, it undergoes a shift toward the erotic. The old film travelogues of the 1930s give way to TV's *The Love Boat* and *Fantasy Island*, where the boat of the former is an instrument not of travel but of liaison, and the fantasies of the latter are not insular but sexual.

It is otherwise with sports and the media. There, too, a shift has occurred, from active participation to the vicarious participation of spectatorship. Four people used to go bowling, but 100 million watch the Superbowl. Football, where men try to hit and hurt, has replaced baseball as the national game. It is as if the demotion from participant to spectatorship and from live spectatorship to TV spectatorship has to be compensated by upping the ante in violence.

The passivity of TV and film watching contrasts with the violence with which the watcher identifies.

The two most popular film stars in the world are Clint Eastwood and Charles Bronson. Each kills a great many

people in each movie, the former casually, the latter by way
of revenge.

Scene from *A Few Dollars More*: Clint Eastwood is a
bounty hunter who is after a wanted man for the reward.
As he closes in on his quarry in a saloon, three friends of the
wanted man come to the latter's rescue. Clint Eastwood kills
all four without changing expression. This pleases us, even
though Eastwood, unlike Ulysses or John Wayne, is killing
just for money.

Recreational drugs offer a spectacular remedy to the disappointed self. Rock star to his chauffeur: "Don't let anybody
kid you—nothing, not sex, not music, not adulation, can compare with the rush of intravenous Dilaudid." There are only
these contraindications: expense, crime, illness, death.

There remains sex as the recreational mainstay, the cheapest, most available, and most pleasurable of recreational options. By "sex" let us specify the entire spectrum of the
erotic, from the "romantic" encounter—cool Audrey Hep-
burn meeting testy Cary Grant by accident when their dogs'
leashes get entangled on the Left Bank—to the cruising
homosexual fellating his five hundredth stranger in Buena
Vista Park.

The mystery of the erotic is that it seems to be proof
against the disappointments of other sectors of life and to
transformation by the media. Travel may be eroticized by
the media, but the erotic is never travelized.

Compare the disappointment of ordinary social life, the
traditional recreation of society, with the erotic encounter.

Scene in one thousand movies: a party, formal stuffed-shirt
party, NYC cocktail party, country club party, New Year's
Eve party, hippie party—any kind of party—but with the one
common denominator of a failed festival, a collapsed and fragmented community. There is always the painfully perceived
gap between what is and what might be. If there were such a

device as a social-relationship indicator and one could quantify the relationship what-is/what-might-be, most parties would register less than 5 percent. Hence the booze. Unlike the use of spirits in the past, the purpose of alcohol is not to celebrate the festival but to anesthetize the failure of the festival. The locus of the failure is the self. Accordingly, the subject to be anesthetized is the self. Richard Pryor: Why free-basing? Because it wipes out the self.

But then at the party, the failed festival, one meets the eye of who else but a stranger and where else but across a crowded room. Eye contact, as the pathognomonic expression of the times goes, is maintained one tenth of a second longer than socially prescribed. It is enough. One approaches. A conversation takes place. Its chief characteristic is that, no matter how banal it is, it is charged with significance.

> I feel that I know you.
> I don't think.
> I feel that I do. Do you know what I mean?
> Yes.

The social-relationship indicator would jump to 95 percent.

The exit line in another one thousand movies: Why don't we get out of here—I know a little Italian restaurant around the corner.

Change of scene: from a failed festival to the last remaining unfailed festival of the twentieth century: the erotic encounter.

A quiet place. Two glasses of wine. Now the alcohol celebrates the festival: The music? Perhaps the Muzak of the cocktail lounge, but it sounds like the dancing violins of Mozart. A touch of arm to arm. A brush of knee against knee. An arrangement: Could you meet me at— A liaison . . .

The sex and violence in Western life, especially American

life, are commonplaces. But the important questions do not have commonplace answers. For example: What is the relation between the two? Are they merely, as one so often hears, the paired symptoms of a decaying society like the fifth-century Roman Empire? Or is there a reciprocal relationship? That is to say, is a thoroughly eroticized society less violent and a thoroughly violent society less erotic?

Or, the more ominous question: Suppose the erotic is the last and best recourse of the stranded self and suppose then that, through the sexual revolution, recreational sex becomes available to all ages and all classes. What if then even the erotic becomes devalued? What if it happens, as Paul Ricoeur put it, that, "at the same time that sexuality becomes insignificant, it becomes more imperative as a response to the disappointments experienced in other sectors of human life"?

What then? Does the self simply diminish, subside into apathy like laboratory animals deprived of sensory stimulation? Or does the demoniac spirit of the self, frustrated by the failure of Eros, turn in the end to the cold fury of Saturn?

It is no longer open to Clint Eastwood to do what Cary Grant did. In fact, Eastwood's character, Dirty Harry, doesn't like girls. But he has his .44 Magnum.

Will the bumper stickers of the 1990s read *Make Love Not War* or *Love Is Gone but War Remains*?

Hold on, says the reader. Just a minute.
Yes?
Are there not plenty of good people left? decent folk who have no truck with what you call the spirit of the erotic and the spirit of violence? millions of people, in fact, such as those described by Charles Kuralt on the road in America who are without exception good, kind, neighborly, generous, patriotic folk?

I am willing to believe it, but where do all the child molesters come from? Look out for benign types like Charlie Kuralt.

And are there not millions of ordinary American families with hardworking devoted husbands, loving wives, good kids, who live happy lives, have a good time without promiscuous sex, drugs, or violence, and on the whole turn out well?

Undoubtedly. In fact, I am amazed how extraordinarily nice most young people are, extraordinarily nice and extraordinarily ignorant.

And don't some people fall in love with their heart's desire, marry, and live reasonably happy lives?

Some. For a while. Maybe. I can't say.

Don't you believe in love?

Yes, but the word has been polluted. Beware of people who go around talking about loving and caring.

And are there not plenty of sincerely religious folk left, Christians and Jews, whose lives are filled with the joy of the love of God and who go about doing good?

Perhaps. Some, I suppose.

And are there not still religious folk, women who give their very lives to serve God and their fellowman, all for the love of God?

Well, some—though for every Mother Teresa, there seem to be 1,800 nutty American nuns, female Clint Eastwoods who have it in for men and are out to get the Pope.

Then what are you saying beyond the commonplace that there are now, just as there have always been, "good" people and "bad" people; or, if you prefer, people with traditional value systems and people with new life styles?

I am only trying to make sense of a peculiar phenomenon, hardly to be ignored: the sudden and unprecedented appearance of florid sexual behavior and the overt and covert practice of violence to the point of rendering cities unlivable, of

nice people like Europeans and Americans killing each other
by the millions—and with it, the very real possibility for the
first time in history that we may destroy ourselves in the near
future.

Decency is as may be, but decent or not, the autonomous
self is devolving upon what seems to it a simple and reasonable view of sexuality. In view of its low cost and availability, the easy prevention of disease and pregnancy, could
anything seem more reasonable than that the traditional
Judaeo-Christian strictures against premarital and extramarital
sex are anachronisms—especially the former in view of the
fact that teenagers are at the height of their sexual powers?
Even the good, gray *New York Times* takes it for granted.
In an editorial protesting certain criticisms of the availability
of contraceptive devices to teenagers without parental consent, the *Times* editorialist wrote: "Some Americans apparently find emotional satisfaction in encouraging teenagers to
deny or postpone their sexuality. It is a costly fantasy, diverting attention and resources from a real world."

Why indeed postpone or deny the sexuality of teenagers?
Admitting the true state of affairs is surely more honest than
retaining a Christian veneer and practicing the sexual mores
of *Dallas* and *The Love Boat*.

Does it only remain then to pause and wonder how such a
mistaken view of sexuality could have informed the entire
Western world for two thousand years? One needs to speak
plainly here. It is, after all, not a small matter to discard such
a traditional view so casually and so quickly. Nor should one
deceive oneself about the consequences of "correcting" the
mistake.

The deception may come from concealing from oneself
the inevitable nature of sexuality in a post-Christian and
technological society by substituting for the lost god and

the lost commandment such surrogate goals as "responsible" sexuality, "commitment," "sharing," and so on.

These humane and in fact admirable properties of a good sexuality as opposed to a bad sexuality may in fact obtain, but it is necessary to note without prejudice that once sexual behavior is viewed objectively as an option of the autonomous self, it will also be viewed necessarily and quite reasonably as a source of pleasure and a need-satisfaction and as such subject to those techniques of the age by which such satisfactions are best arrived at and with the least damage to others. And why not? Cannot recreational sex be enjoyed responsibly, that is, without damage to one's health or the health of others, physical health and emotional health? One can eat one's cake and have it too. The words *responsibility*, *mutuality*, *sharing*, *caring*, are easily added, the cake's icing.

A SHORT HISTORY OF THE DEMONIAC SPIRIT OF THE EROTIC AND THE VIOLENT IN THE CHRISTIAN ERA, IN THE TRANSITION FROM THE CHRISTIAN ERA TO THE TECHNOLOGICAL ERA, AND FINALLY IN A PURELY TECHNOLOGICAL ERA

St. Paul: The triumph of the spirit over the flesh, but still bothered by a "thorn in the flesh" (unlike Socrates, who wouldn't have worried).

St. Augustine: The triumph of the love of God in the City of God over lust in the city of man, but—"Grant me the gift of continence, but not just yet."

Dante: Sexual sinners in the outermost, least punitive, circle of hell, storm-tossed, blown to and fro like birds on the winds of desire, yet still together and still in love. Cf. traitors and murderers in innermost circle, up to their necks in boiling pitch.

Chaucer's Miller and Wife of Bath: The frankly erotic harmonized comically and humanely as earthy transgressions, committed and recognized as sins, but without neurotic guilt and to be forgiven by the loving Lord and Master, the goal of the Canterbury pilgrimage.

Don Giovanni: The appearance of the pure demoniac spirit of the erotic; the Don's seduction of 1,003 women set to the joyful music of Mozart; yet this same spirit of the erotic posited by Christianity, e.g., the damnation of the Don and his descent before our eyes into the fires of hell.

Fanny Hill: The spirit of the erotic in English pornography; the sinister charm of secret sex under the veneer of Christian proprieties and layers of Victorian clothes; the white skin of thighs against black stockings.

World War I: Joyce Kilmer's poetry, Colleen Moore in *Lilac Time*, "Mademoiselle from Armentières"; the erotic diminished to the sentimental and to good-natured sex between the doughboy and the French farm girl; with a decline in passion and the spirit of the erotic, and an increase in violence with the rise in technology; 20,000,000 dead.

World War II: Betty Grable, Anne Frank, Adolf Eichmann, Stalin; the subsidence of the erotic in favor of a rise in the dispassionate, abstract violence of ideology, Fascism, Nazism, Communism; war increasingly in the hands of technicians; the decency of Truman and Oppenheimer contrasted with the death of 100,000 women and children in Hiroshima and Nagasaki; Arendt's banality of evil = the growing disparity between the monstrous violence of technology and the smallness of the technician-perpetrators; World War II as a transition period between the decline of the Christian era and the rise of the age of technology; 50,000,000 dead.

Period between World War II and World War III: The ascendancy of the erotic; the eroticization of all sectors of culture: work and play, films, TV, novels, plays, commercials; yet the spirit of the erotic is still posited and specified by lingering Christianity, e.g., the charm of the secrecy of sex under clothes, the charm of "forbidden" sex, liaisons, pornography; pornography as "dirty" yet interesting, or rather, "dirty," therefore interesting; the hypocrisy of some critics: critics who say that pornography is dull, whereas in fact pornography is for many readers the last resort of interest after the disappointments of age; the critic, of all people, knows that the non-pornographic novel is generally so boring that he hopes for the "dirty part" like a schoolboy looking for the "good parts" of *Ulysses*.

The spirit of violence vented in spectatorship sport, either through mass TV viewership or surrogate participation, e.g., 100 million people watching the Superbowl; Little League moms screaming curses at umpires, and dads punching out other dads and later beating up their own kids; the ultimate inadequacy of the spectatorship safety valve: thirty-eight dead in a riot at a Buenos Aires soccer game; war.

World War III: The year 2000+, the demoniac spirit of the erotic no longer posited by Christianity but triumphant in its own right, perfected as genital technique but deprived of the charm of the forbidden, the secret, the "dirty," "sinful," "extramarital," "fornication," "adultery"—even the word *fuck* has by now lost its homonymous semantic charge and is as neutered as *fish, fowl, fix;* the perfection of contraceptive technique; the conquest of Herpes II virus and all homosexual "aids" diseases; the perfection of visual and tactile aids (no longer called pornography, from *porne,* harlot) as sexual stimuli; erotica elevated to a major literary and art form. War without passion: one billion dead.

The spirit of violence in the coming technological sexually liberated age? Here is the great problematic.

Question (The Great Problematic): Will the ultimate libera-
tion of the erotic from its dialectical relationship with Christianity result in

(*a*) The freeing of the erotic spirit so that man- and
womankind will make love and not war?

or (*b*) The trivialization of the erotic by its demotion to
yet another technique and need-satisfaction of the organism,
toward the end that the demoniac spirit of the autonomous
self, disappointed in all other sectors of life and in ordinary
intercourse with others, is now disappointed even in the
erotic, its last and best hope, and so erupts in violence—and
in that very violence which is commensurate with the orgastic
violence in the best days of the old erotic age—i.e., war?

(CHECK ONE)

Question II:

(*a*) Will World War III happen absurdly, by an accident
in a purely technological, sexually liberated age, e.g., by
computer malfunction, misinformation, misbehavior by a
small-time Qaddafi madman?

or (*b*) Will World War III erupt because of the sup-
pressed fury of the autonomous self, disappointed now even
in the erotic, that very demoniac spirit which is overtly committed to peace and love but secretly desires war and apocalypse and nourishes hatred of all other selves and perhaps of
its own self most of all?

(CHECK ONE)

THE BESTIAL-SEXUAL

Thought Experiment: The Confrontation of the Autonomous
Scientific Self with the Eruption of the Spirit of the Erotic,

Issuing in Two Kinds of Violence, one the Bestial-Sexual, the other the Banal-Lethal

Scene I: Open house at the Maison Burgundy, a French Quarter hotel in New Orleans, celebrating Mental Health Week, open to the public and hosted by mental-health workers, psychiatrists, psychologists, social workers, et al.

The most popular hostess is "Dr. Betty," a visiting radio "personality," a nationally known talk-show psychotherapist (known in the business as a "psych jock"), a pleasant, fortyish blonde just this side of the overblown and overweight, but in an attractive, even voluptuous, way. A small crowd has gathered around her. She fields questions in her best low-keyed, cheerful radio style.

Someone, a thin intense young woman, has just asked a question about how to overcome sexual inhibitions: "I like men, they like me, I want a rewarding sexual relationship, but I turn myself off," etc.

One of the listeners in the small crowd is a young street person known hereabouts as a "chicken," that is, a teenage male prostitute available to either sex. Streetwise, somehow managing to swagger standing still, in his short leather jacket he looks like a muscular, coarse, slightly out-of-focus John Travolta. While the others smile and nod, he stands, thumbs hooked through his belt loops, and watches Dr. Betty through hooded eyes.

Dr. Betty: Give yourself permission! Speak to yourself, you're an adult—not some other adult—speak to the child in you: Kid, I give you permission. None of us likes to be stroke-deficient. We live by strokes. That means taking care of the child in us. My child, your child, likes to play. And sex, of course, is our primary stroke-field. Sex is the best play of all. And the best sex is when two mature adults, who are both nurturing and caring of each other, are also nurturing and caring of their own child-selves, their own kid—and who regard each other as their primary stroke-field. There you have the ultimate recipe for happiness, growth, and creativity. It's in my book, *Dr. Betty's Favorite Recipe*.

Laughter and nods all around—except from the street chicken, who waits until the others leave. He approaches Dr. Betty, motions her to a corner of the lobby. "Yes?" says Dr. Betty brightly.

CHICKEN: Look, Doc. I'm a big fan of yours. I think you're great. You know your business and you're good. But I know my business just as well. I can size people up. I know what people want. And believe me, Doc, everybody wants something. I know what you want. You're a nice person and you deserve it.

DR. BETTY (*bantering*): And what do I want?

CHICKEN: You want exactly what I'm offering. I know the clerk here. I got a key and the use of a room. Look. Four thirty-seven. It won't cost either of us a dime. I'm going up now. You wait five minutes and come up the back elevator.

DR. BETTY: This is something else. Talk about acting out! Talk about acting out aggressions to mask little-kid insecurity. Okay, then what happens?

CHICKEN: What happens then, Doc, is that I am going to fuck you as you have never been fucked before. I don't want to nurture you. I want to fuck you. I'm going to fuck you till your eyeteeth rattle. This is an invitation, Doc. All you got to do now before I leave is say okay, so I don't waste my time.

DR. BETTY (*consulting her wristwatch*): Okay.

The Banal-Lethal

SCENE II: A Washington hotel room. It is wartime. Enter Dr. F———, a Nobel Laureate scientist. Taking off his jacket, he sits on the bed wearily, rubs his temples, lies down, and closes his eyes. After a while, he turns on television. The show is a closed-circuit screening of *Behind the Green Door*, a pornographic film. Presently he masturbates, almost casually, but not before taking the trouble to fetch a special container from his suitcase to catch the ejaculate.

He switches off the television, lies down, closes his eyes.

The telephone rings. With a frown and a curious groan— is it weariness? irritation? anger?—he picks up the receiver. After a moment he hooks up a device, a scrambler, to the phone. We hear only his side of the conversation.

Yes.

Yes, General.

Yes, it was a very long meeting.

I realize that a decision wasn't reached.

I know it's important, General.

True, there was no closure in the decision-making process.

Yes, I realize it was a tie vote.

That's correct—I didn't express an opinion to the Chiefs.

Yes, that's true. I have some standing in the scientific community.

Well, thank you, General. It's nice to know you people respect one scientist.

That's right, General. It's no breach of security to call it by name. The eyes-only folder you have—and the only secret is its composition and mode of delivery. It's a neurotoxin, airborne and water soluble. They're working on it, too.

For one weapon? Ten million more or less, depending on population density.

Right. It violates no first-strike agreement or Salt III. It's a weapon, but not an explosive device.

I know that's a high civilian casualty factor, but it will save lives in the end.

A demonstration? A demonstration of what? How to kill a few hundred reindeer in Siberia? No way, General.

You're really putting me on the spot, General.

Okay, I'm going to surprise you. I'm going to give you an opinion. I think we got to go with it. For the ultimate good of man. Indeed, in the interests of peace. In fact, why don't we call it Project Peace?

You like that? Yes, that's right. Go. You can tell them.

I say go.

After hanging up, he picks up the cylindrical double-walled container, carefully pastes on a sticker containing the address of a California laboratory which collects the sperm of Nobel Laureates for the purpose of inseminating thousands of genetically screened women. Still holding the container, he opens the door, walks rapidly down the corridor to the ice machine.

Question: Do you think the U.S. gene pool and the future quality of life will be improved by the contribution of Dr. F——'s ejaculate?

( ) Yes
( ) No

(CHECK ONE)

SCENE III: The following conversation occurs in a momentarily stalled elevator in the Rockefeller Foundation building.

SCIENTIST A (*a post-Darwinian evolutionist*): All phenomena in the Cosmos can be explained by the scientific laws that govern matter in interaction. This principle applies to the simplest chemical reaction between atoms to the most complex, including the behavior of organisms, the origin of the species, and the ascent of man. Like any other organism, man evolved when mutant forms and functions such as the opposable thumb for tools and weapons, the cortex, and the larynx-pharynx conformation for language gave him an advantage over other primates in adapting to the environment.

SCIENTIST B (*a post-Wallacian evolutionist*): Then how do you account for the fact that with the appearance of man there also appeared for the first time in the Cosmos, as far as we know, language, mind, self, and consciousness, and almost immediately thereafter a train of disasters and triumphs which seem to have very little to do with adapting to an environment—such as organized warfare against himself, composing *Don Giovanni*, Charlie Manson, John Keats, suicide, joy, madness, murder, heroism, modern medicine, child abuse, loving care for the genetically malformed—and in recent years the appearance of the demoniac spirit of the erotic and the violent expressing itself in every conceivable variety of florid sexual behavior which has nothing to do with reproduction or survival of the species, and that with the very rise of science there has occurred the spectacular rise in technological violence, so that more men have been killed in this century than in all others put together—and that finally there should have come to pass the present state of affairs which surpass all belief, not merely that this very "matter" you speak of, which Democritus and Darwin and even Dalton and Boyle saw as peaceable little miniballs of atoms colliding and joining, is in fact possessed of an energy of such an order that one-quarter teaspoon will destroy Greater New York, but that this very secret and this very matter—and here the mind reels—should find itself in the hands of this selfsame demoniac autonomous self, itself a creature of science?

Scientist *A* opens his mouth to reply, but the elevator doors open at last and there enters a somber-looking Hasidic rabbi. The two scientists exchange glances and fall silent.

Question: How do you think Scientist *A* would have answered Scientist *B*?

A SPACE ODYSSEY
(I)

(19) The Self Marooned in the Cosmos: *What would you say if you met a man Friday out there? What do you think he would say to you? Could you understand him?*

A starship from earth is traveling in the galaxy, its mission to establish communication with extraterrestrial intelligences and civilizations.*

For years SETI (Search for Extraterrestrial Intelligence) has explored the 200 billion stars of the galaxy, huge dish antennae searching for something, anything other than the random noise of the Cosmos. At last, the computer of the spectrum analyzer which reads the tapes of all the received transmissions picked up a pattern, that is, a repeated signal,

---

* This chapter, as well as other parts of the book, owes a good deal to Carl Sagan's splendid picture book, *Cosmos*. I hope he will not take offense at some fanciful extrapolations therefrom. Sagan's book gave me much pleasure, a pleasure which was not diminished (perhaps was even increased) by Sagan's unmalicious, even innocent, scientism, the likes of which I have not encountered since the standard bull sessions of high school and college— up to but not past the sophomore year. The argument could be resumed with Sagan, I suppose, but the issue would be as inconclusive as it was between sophomores. For me it was more diverting than otherwise to see someone sketch the history of Western scientific thought and leave out Judaism and Christianity. Everything is downhill after the Ionians and until the rise of modern science. There is a huge gap between the destruction of the library at Alexandria and the appearance of Copernicus and Galileo. So much for six thousand years of Judaism and fifteen hundred years of Christianity. So much for the likes of Aristotle, Hippocrates, Galen, Aquinas, Roger Bacon, Grosseteste. So much for the science historian A. C. Crombie, who wrote: "The natural philosophers of Latin Christendom in the thirteenth and fourteenth centuries created the experimental science characteristic of modern times."

So much, indeed, for the relationship between Christianity and science and the fact that, as Whitehead pointed out, it is no coincidence that science sprang, not from Ionian metaphysics, not from the Brahmin-

which, however, could not be interpreted. Was it a signal from an intelligence or was it like the Coke bottle in the movie *On the Beach*, which was leaning on a telegraph key in deserted California and which a fitful breeze blowing a curtain caused to send out a random letter or two?

The starship has a transmission-receiver capability for the entire electromagnetic spectrum, but especially in the range of radio signals, since it is known of course that the Cosmos is filled with emissions in this part of the spectrum, from pulsars, quasars, radiation belts, and so on.

Buddhist-Taoist East, not from the Egyptian-Mayan astrological South, but from the heart of the Christian West, that although Galileo fell out with the Church, he would hardly have taken so much trouble studying Jupiter and dropping objects from towers if the reality and value and order of things had not first been conferred by belief in the Incarnation.

Yet one is not offended by Sagan. There is too little malice and too much ignorance. It is enough to take pleasure in the pleasant style, the knack for popularizing science, and the beautiful pictures of Saturn and the Ring Nebula.

Indeed, more often than not, I found myself on Sagan's side, especially in his admiration for science and the scientific method, which is what he says it is—a noble, elegant, and self-correcting method of attaining a kind of truth—and when he attacks the current superstitions, astrology, UFOs, parapsychology, and such, which seem to engage the Western mind now more than ever—more perhaps than either science or Christianity.

What is to be deplored is not Sagan's sophomoric scientism—which I think I like better than its counterpart, a sophomoric theism which attributes the wonders of the Cosmos to a God who created it like a child with a cookie cutter—no, what is deplorable is that these serious issues involving God and the nature of man should be co-opted by the present disputants, a popularizer like Sagan and fundamentalists who believe God created the world six thousand years ago. It's enough to give both science and Christianity a bad name.

Really, it is a case of an ancient and still honorable argument going to pot. Even arguments in a college dormitory are, or were, conducted at a higher level.

It is for this very reason that we can enjoy *Cosmos* so much, for the frivolity of Sagan's vulgar scientism and for the reason that science is, as Sagan says, self-correcting. One wonders, in fact, whether Sagan himself has not been corrected, e.g., by Hubble's discovery of the red shift and the present growing consensus of the Big Bang theory of the creation of the Cosmos, which surely comes closer than Sagan would like to the Genesis account of *creatio ex nihilo*.

The objective of the starship is to exchange information with other civilizations comparable with or superior to our own. It has been calculated that the probability that such civilizations exist is overwhelming. What the designers of the project hoped to learn was the level of technology of other civilizations, the degree of evolution, biology, type of metabolism, etc.

The time is the year 2050 C.E. (Common Era, so called because, though the era is post-Christian, it proved useful to retain the year of Christ's birth). The acceleration of vehicles to speeds approaching the speed of light is possible, the aging process is accordingly reduced, and the problems of communication delays are minimized.

The assumption was made that as organisms evolve in the Cosmos, a level of intelligence will be reached so that it will be possible to transmit information. Mathematics and science might be used as the basis of a common language. Mathematics is the same everywhere. The prime numbers 1, 2, 3, 5, 7, 11, 13 . . . are prime everywhere. The physics of the Cosmos is the same. For example, since hydrogen is the most abundant atom in the Cosmos, one might use the proton and electron spin of the neutral hydrogen atom as the binary number 1. Using such a binary system, the project designers hoped that it might be possible to establish a vocabulary and transmit information about the earth and its star, for example, its position in relation to the fourteen major pulsars of the galaxy, and to put similar questions to other intelligences.

Organisms transmitting signals were, in fact, encountered. The trouble was that the responses received were not acknowledgments or statements of information but were rather countersignals of one sort or another, responses which seemed to express something like excitement or alarm or anger, often actual movements of the organisms themselves. Thus, rather

than information being obtained, various behaviors were encountered—hostile, aversive, coming close or going away,
flight or fight, and in one case what appeared to be an attempt
at sexual union.

In fact, two such creatures were encountered in the solar
system.

(1) In the outer atmosphere of Jupiter, large gaseous
clouds were sighted. It was determined that they were self-
contained organisms of some intelligence because they were
self-propelled, moving about by emitting jets of hydrogen.
They injested organic molecules and excreted helium and
methane, and were observed to reproduce by fission. But
despite every effort to communicate, e.g., by transmitting
prime numbers in various frequencies of the electromagnetic
spectrum, the only response of the clouds was to speed away
or come close and surround the ship like a sportive school of
whales—or to rise and sink like so many hot-air balloons.

(2) Skirting Saturn's moon Titan with its heavy atmosphere of methane, another sort of creature was encountered,
small glittering anemone-like organisms with spicules of
methane crystals and a beak-and-sucker mouth for devouring
the brown sludge of organic molecules formed on Titan's
surface by the ultraviolet light of the sun. Upon the transmission of radio waves of the frequency 1420 megahertz,
the creatures were thrown into violent excitement, for all the
world like the behavior of male gypsy moths upon the reception of the female pheromone. They flocked to the ship and
attached themselves to its tiles and windows, using their
sucker-like mouths. It was not clear whether such a response
was a manifestation of hunger or hostility or an attempt at
sexual union.

At last, five years later, near Proxima Centauri, communication was established with an extraterrestrial intelligence.

Orbiting the third planet of Proxima Centauri (PC3), of PC's twelve planets the one most resembling Earth, the earthship transmitted the prime numbers in the radio range of the electromagnetic spectrum. Almost immediately, the signal was returned—and imitated. But when the excited earthlings tried to descend, a glitch occurred in the controls, not once, but repeatedly—until it finally dawned on the crew that they were being held in orbit. Evidently, the earthship was being detained at a kind of checkpoint until its credentials were approved.

It was necessary to hit upon a mathematical and semantic vocabulary. The former was easy, again using the physical properties of the hydrogen atom, assigning the binary number 1 to the transition between the parallel and antiparallel proton and electron spins of the neutral hydrogen atom. Such a transition emits a radio-frequency photon of wavelength 21 centimeters and a frequency of 1420 megahertz—the reason for selecting this channel of transmission. An indexical lexicon was agreed upon. Thus, certain binary numbers were assigned to the suns of Centauri by transmitting the number along with the angle or declination of the suns from the path of transmission. Similarly, other names were assigned to other features, the other referents being "pointed at" and "named," e.g., light, dark, other planets, pulsars, big, little, red, blue, near, far, down, up, here, there, I (the earthship), you (PC3), and so on. Plurals and abstractions and tenses were agreed upon. Goodness was a property attributed to cosmic particles which were beneficial to the metabolism of the PC3 organisms, evil to the ultraviolet rays, which were harmful. Even metaphor was arrived at: *I am M4 today*, meaning I am your fourth moon, PC3's fourth moon being bright, small, racy, refractile as a diamond. Or *I am M6*— sluggish, blue, misshapen, bored. Consciousness was defined as that property of a creature by which he draws attention to something, talks about it, or thinks about it. It was designated by a binary number which we shall call C.

A lexicon and syntax agreed upon, it was now possible for the earthship to transmit basic information about its origin, its sun, the geology, atmosphere, age of the planet earth, the biology of its organisms (e.g., C, H, O, S, H_2O, PO_4; deoxyribonucleic acid; mobile heterotrophs; surface dwellers; O_2 breathers; sexual mammals, etc.), its technology (nuclear energic), its culture (two hundred nation-states, five global powers, sporadic brushfire warfare, environmental pollution), its science, its art (literary, iconic, musical)—a message ending with a sign-off and an invitation: *Over and out—come back.*

There followed a long pause, then an explicit warning: *Maintain orbit until certain questions are answered*—then the transmission of a binary symbol which the earthlings translated as something like the Hebrew *shalom*—then the transmission of comparable summary of PC3 information, indicating an organism with a bromine metabolism, an older civilization than that of Earth, and a superior technology (exponentiating, approaching asymptotic limit). Culture: global, gregarious, 40,000 genera, one symbolic language(!) (cf. Earth's thousands), reproduction: sexual(!), biology: non-senescent(!): did that mean they did not age or die?!???; art: mathematical-poetic.

There then followed several transmissions from PC3 which the earthlings did not understand. They were

T, Si → Sy = 1.35 × 10^{12} years (breakthrough)
Si = atmospheric wave motion, tactile, radar return
Sy = variable pitch frequencies combined with radar-return configurations, or SRs (sound-radar)

$$Sn = SR_1 + SR_2 \ (+ = \text{assert})$$
$$C = 1 \ (\text{Int, Soc, Sy})$$

Each item of information was followed by the query: "What's yours?" Then: "What's your C-type? Are you C1? C2? C3? Over and out. Come back."

A puzzled silence from the earthship transmitter, then: "Say again." Then: "Say again longer [i.e., Explain]. What is C-type? What is Si? Sy? Si → Sy breakthrough? T? Sn?

After many weeks of transmissions, dogged human effort, and an unflagging good-humored patience from the PC3 transmitter, the following explanations were spelled out:

$$T = \text{time}$$
$$Si = \text{sign}$$
$$Sy = \text{symbol}$$
$$Sn = \text{sentence}$$

T, Si → Sy 1.35×10^{12} years means how long ago in PC3 years we made the breakthrough from sign communication to symbol communication, i.e., 13,500,000 years.

Before that, we communicated by touch, sounds of different pitches, and a radar-like reception of reflected sound. Like a bat, said an earthling. Imagine bats flying blind and emitting squeaks of different musical pitches.

Sy, or symbols, were formed by combining frequency clusters (e.g., chords of musical squeaks) with the percept or radar configuration formed by the radar-return of this or that object. Thus, instead of the word *ball* being applied to the round thing you earthlings play with, our primitive word was applied to the jagged radar-configuration of the double-bladed sickle with which our ancestors harvested our atmospheric algae. Our "words" or symbols are combinations of musical chords (for objects), arpeggios (for action words, verbs) with the corresponding radar percepts, just as your words *ball, yellow, slice* are combinations of sound configurations and visual percepts (though we don't quite understand what you mean by "visual" and "see").

Sn is a sentence, uniting two of these sound-radar configurations, so:

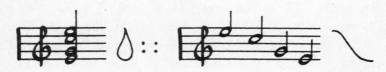

means: Your spaceship is descending.

EARTHSHIP: True. Very interesting. We read. Request permission to land. We could exchange much more information by meeting and talking.

PC3: Not quite yet. You haven't answered our question about C-type.

EARTHSHIP: What do you mean by type of consciousness?

PC3: We are C_1s. We wanted to know whether you are C_1s or C_2s or C_3s.

EARTHSHIP: What is a C_1?

PC3 (*patiently*): We told you. $C = 1$ (Int, Soc, Sy).

EARTHSHIP: What does that mean?

PC3 (*patiently*): It means that in order for the individual consciousness to be activated, it is required that there be a *Soc*, that is, a society, that is, two or more persons; an exchange of *Sy*, that is, symbols; and an *Int*, that is, an intersubjective relationship in which there is agreement about the symbol used and the thing that is talked about.

EARTHSHIP: Oh.

PC3: And you?

EARTHSHIP: We're much the same. Now may we request permission to—

PC3: Just a moment. It is still necessary to establish your C-type. We are C1s, that is, first-order consciousness. Through the centuries we have learned by painful experience that there are at least two other C-types, C2s and C3s. C1s and C3s are benign. C2s are dangerous. Which are you?

EARTHSHIP: Say again. What's the difference?

PC3: A C1 consciousness is a first-order consciousness, or what you would call a preternatural consciousness—according to the dictionary your computer transmitted.

EARTHSHIP: It is? Say again. Preternatural?

PC3: Well, something like the consciousness of a child grown mature and sophisticated but maintaining its innocence permanently and avoiding the malformations of self-consciousness, enjoying the beauty of our planet and each other and our science and art without weariness, boredom, fear, guilt, or shame. Like what you call the Helen Keller phenomenon.

EARTHSHIP: How do you know about her?

PC3: One of our cosmological linguists just arrived. This is he speaking. We've been monitoring you for years. Switch to Earth-L, English-speaking? German? French?

EARTHSHIP: American English.

PC3: Got it. I read. What can we do for you?

EARTHSHIP: What do you mean by the Helen Keller phenomenon?

PC3: The joy of consciousness and the discovery of the Cosmos through the mediation of symbols and the cooperation of others and the preservation of this joy against the incursions of boredom, fear, anger, despair, shame, and the love of war and death and the secret desire for the misfortune of others.

EARTHSHIP: Check. Did you say shame?

PC3: We have observed that C2s experience shame. For example, do you wear clothes?

EARTHSHIP: Yes.

PC3: Despite the controlled environment of your ship?

EARTHSHIP: Yes.

PC3: Why?

EARTHSHIP: Ah, custom. Aesthetics.

PC3: Aesthetics? Explain.

EARTHSHIP: Later, when we land. May we land?

PC3: Not yet. What is your C-type?

EARTHSHIP: What is a C2 consciousness?

PC3: A C2 consciousness is a consciousness which passes through a C1 stage and then for some reason falls into the pit of itself.

EARTHSHIP: The pit of itself?

PC3: In some evolving civilizations, for reasons which we don't entirely understand, the evolution of consciousness is attended by a disaster of some sort which occurs shortly after the *Sy* breakthrough. It has something to do with the discovery of the self and the incapacity to deal with it, the consciousness becoming self-conscious but not knowing what to do with the self, not even knowing what its self is, and so ending by being that which it is not, saying that which is not, doing that which is not, and making others what they are not.

EARTHSHIP: What does that mean?

PC3: Playing roles, being phony, lying, cheating, stealing, and killing. To say nothing of exotic disordering of the reproductive apparatus of sexual creatures.

EARTHSHIP: What does that mean?

PC3: Exploitative sex.

EARTHSHIP: Exploitative sex?

PC3 (*consulting computerized earth-slang dictionary*): It seems to mean what you call "screwing everything in sight," not only ♂ to ♀ and ♀ to ♂ but ♂ to ♂ and ♀ to ♀ and

♂ + ♀ + ♀ and ♀ + ♂ + ♂—to mention a few of the simpler combinations.

EARTHSHIP: That is what is called "freedom of sexual preference."

PC3: Call it what you like. We are not interested. What concerns us is our experience with C2s whom we have allowed to land on PC3. They are usually polite at first, but always turn hostile, deceptive, and end by attempting to screw (is that the right word?) any creatures on PC3 which have an opening or a protuberance. We could tolerate their odd sexual behavior, but they were also sentimental and cruel—or rather sentimental, therefore cruel. One goes with the other. They are mainly interested in self-esteem. We are afraid of C2s. They do not know themselves or what to do with themselves.

EARTHSHIP: What about you? What do you do about your consciousness and your selves?

PC3: That is no problem. For us, consciousness of self is no different from consciousness of anything else. A self here is an individual self yet also a self among other selves. C2 selves vary from moment to moment from self-grandiosity to self-refusal, from being the infinite great self in the world to being the worst and the least self—because C2 selves don't know who they are.* Perhaps your difficulty comes from the sensory mode which you call "seeing." You "see" things. But can you "see" yourself? Who are you?

---

* A C1 consciousness is selfless, the PC3 earthologist went on to say, unaware of self, because it is looking out, seeing things, and symbolizing through intersubjective transactions with others. Perhaps the C1 consciousness of an earthling two-year-old at the time of the explosive acquisition of language is an ontogenetic recapitulation of a species of consciousness possessed by the ice-age man who painted the caves of the Dordogne.

A C2 consciousness, on the other hand, looks out, sees, and symbolizes but has also become self-conscious. But the self is literally inconceivable—unlike a tree or a star or you, it cannot be conceived under the auspices of

EARTHSHIP: I'm the second officer, the communications officer.

PC3: No, I mean, who are you?

EARTHSHIP: You mean my name? Captain—

PC3 (*patiently*): No. Let's begin with C-type. What's your C-type? Are you C1, C2, or C3? You will not be given permission to descend until we establish that.

EARTHSHIP (*after a pause*): What's a C3 consciousness?

PC3: A C3 consciousness is a C2 consciousness which has become aware of its predicament, sought help, and received it.

EARTHSHIP: Help?

PC3: If a C1 meets with disaster, falls into the pit of itself, and becomes a C2, it must become aware of its sickness and seek a remedy in order to be restored to the preternaturality of C1. Well?

EARTHSHIP: Well what?

PC3: Which are you?

EARTHSHIP: That is hard to say.

PC3: Perhaps we can help you arrive at an answer. Would you answer a few questions?

EARTHSHIP: Yes.

PC3: You say your civilization has five superpowers.

EARTHSHIP: Yes.

PC3: Is there peace between you?

EARTHSHIP: There was when we left.

PC3: Aren't you in communication with Earth?

EARTHSHIP: We were until two years ago.

---

a symbol—and is referentially mobile. That is to say, one's self exists for oneself on a semantic ∝ to − ∝ axis, the best and the worst, the blessed and the damned, and is capable of temporary fixation on any position on this axis.

A C3 consciousness has managed by assistance from something other than self to recover itself from this mobility, through auspices other than symbolic conception, and knows itself for what it is.

PC3: Isn't that strange?

EARTHSHIP: Yes.

PC3: Then you have reason to believe something is wrong on Earth?

EARTHSHIP: Yes. (*Quickly*) Do you know anything?

PC3 (*evasively*): Let's get on with the questions. How many wars have you had in the last hundred earth-years?

EARTHSHIP: Big or little?

PC3: Well, big.

EARTHSHIP: Two—that we know of. Do you know of a third?

PC3: How many lives were terminated before their natural C_2 deaths?

EARTHSHIP: You mean how many were killed?

PC3: Yes.

EARTHSHIP: Around a hundred million.

PC3: Now you fear there might have been a third.

EARTHSHIP: Yes. Do you know?

PC3: What is the size of your crew?

EARTHSHIP: Twelve in the beginning.

PC3: How many of each sex?

EARTHSHIP: Six.

PC3: How did you arrive at the sexual distribution?

EARTHSHIP: We felt that sexual needs must be taken into account, just like the needs for food, water, a stable environment, and so on. And though none of us has any prejudice against homosexuality, we were not yet sure enough of the dynamics of a homosexual group to take chances with the mission.

PC3: Is there pair bonding among you?

EARTHSHIP: No. Ours was designed as a communal and transcultural group interaction. Through extensive prelaunch exercises, we discovered we could get beyond the usual cultural and sexual hang-ups.

PC3: How has it worked?

EARTHSHIP: Among the nine survivors, very well until just recently.

PC3: Nine survivors? What happened to the other three?

EARTHSHIP (*after a silence*): They died.

PC3: Were they killed?

EARTHSHIP: Yes.

PC3: Were they men?

EARTHSHIP: Yes.

PC3: Were they killed in quarrels over the women?

EARTHSHIP: Yes. How did you know?

PC3: We've had some experience with C2s. How are things now?

EARTHSHIP: Fine. Each man has two women. We think we've made a valuable contribution to prolonged heterosexual group dynamics.

PC3: What's that?

EARTHSHIP: Men are less monogamous than women. Men are happier with more than one woman, and the women don't seem to mind, once they've gotten past cultural hangups.

PC3: Interesting. Now, you say you're the second officer.

EARTHSHIP: Yes.

PC3: Can I speak to the commander?

EARTHSHIP: I'm afraid not.

PC3: You mean, the commander didn't survive.

EARTHSHIP: He survived, but he's, ah, ill.

PC3: What's wrong with him?

EARTHSHIP: He's out of it. Flaked out. He sniffs coke and reads Rod McKuen and Richard Bach. He's not functioning. We need to land. Request permission.

PC3: Did you say two women are assigned to each man?

EARTHSHIP: Not assigned. That's the way it worked out. At first.

PC3: What happened? For example, what about the commander's two women?

EARTHSHIP: They're okay. When he lost interest, they turned to each other. They have a relationship.

PC3: Who is the other officer?

EARTHSHIP: He's the exec.

PC3: What's he doing?

EARTHSHIP: Screwing his brains out.

PC3: What about you?

EARTHSHIP: I'm too damn busy flying this ship. Request—

PC3: Then you're in trouble.

EARTHSHIP: Yes. We have to land before we even consider returning.

PC3: No, I mean your species is in trouble. You don't even know whether you have a civilization, and the chances are you do not.

EARTHSHIP: That is correct.

PC3: My question is this. Clearly, you are a C2. We need to know how you stand vis-à-vis your predicament, that is, knowledge of it and remedy for it. E.g., do you have such knowledge? Have you requested help? Has help arrived? Did you accept help?

EARTHSHIP: Help? What help? We don't ask for help. We help ourselves. We are the triumphant emerging species on our planet, and though we are not as far advanced as you, we are not ashamed of our scientific and technological and artistic achievements. If we were not a tough, self-sufficient, inquisitive species, we wouldn't be here.

PC3: Then help was not requested and has not arrived?

EARTHSHIP: Are you talking about religion? If so, I can only reply that we have progressed beyond sectarianism— which caused many of the troubles you speak of. We have selected many of the values of the World's Great Religions —such as meditation, caring, sharing, interpersonal warmth, creativity—and we have rejected sectarian claims of exclusivity and anthropomorphic gods.

PC3: I see. Any other immediate troubles?

EARTHSHIP: My two women are fighting. Both were thought to be culturally liberated and were so certified by the screening procedure. But one has reverted to the old monogamy and wants the captain to marry us. The other one wants to screw the captain and me at the same time and also run the ship.

(*Sotto voce conversation near PC3 transmitter overheard by earthship officer who has learned a bit of PC linguistics, and of which he can make out only:* "—My God, we need these people like a [*word not understood*]—Get them out of here—")

EARTHSHIP: I'm sure the difficulties of these women are not genetic and would not present a problem for you. One is undergoing a neurotic regression, the other a manic-erotic episode. I'm afraid our screening procedure was inadequate. The goddam shrinks screwed up as usual.

PC3 (*sorrowfully*): Permission denied. Please resume your mission or return.

EARTHSHIP (*frantically*): We can't return. There is nothing to return to.

PC3: That is correct. I suggest you proceed to PC7, which is also a C2 civilization. You can take your chances with each other. They, too, are a curious, inquisitive, murderous civilization, NH₃ breathers, nuclear, but not as advanced as you. They are sentimental, easily moved to tears, and kill each other with equal ease. Uncognitive of their predicament and pre-help. Paranoid mind-set. Two superpowers, ideological combat but not yet a nuclear exchange. They like wars too, pretend not to, but get in trouble during an overly prolonged peace. Right now they are bored to death and spoiling for a fight. They are divided into two hostile powers. You would be welcomed by either as a sensational diversion—for a while. There would be parades. You might talk one or both parties into permitting your entry, but each will suspect that you are a spy for the other. Good luck. You have one hour to vacate orbit. Over and out.

Question: If you were the second officer on the starship, how would you answer the question: Are you a C_1? a C_2? a C_3?

(*a*) (*Behaviorist speaking*) I give no answer. The question is not meaningful. There is no hard evidence that there is such an entity as consciousness, let alone "three types of consciousness." In the behavioral sciences, we have discovered that we do very well indeed without recognizing such a thing as consciousness; in fact, by so doing, we have avoided the whole can of worms of subjectivity which has plagued psychology for hundreds of years.

(*b*) (*Sagan speaking*) C_1. Our species is not qualitatively different from other creatures, but the evolution of man has been spectacular, from toolmaking hunter-gatherers to conscious technological man—with a few lapses such as the Christian epoch or the Dark Ages, lasting, say, from the destruction of the Alexandria library to the resumption of scientific progress with Galileo. We still have aggressive traits, but these can be explained by our residual reptilian brain. We do not recognize the existence of a "soul" or "psyche" if these entities be interpreted as anything other than a property of the organization of the DNA and other molecules of the organism.

(*c*) (*Oriental, gnostic, etc., speaking*) C_1. We already live in a preternatural state of bliss if we but knew it. Our misery comes from *maya* and our own errors and can be dissipated by our own efforts. No help required or asked for or received.

(*d*) (*Jew speaking*) C_2. Following an original preternatural or Edenic state, man did indeed suffer a catastrophe or Fall through his own pride and his own choice made in his God-given freedom. In his original state he invented language, named creatures, loved God and his mate, and was happy in his beautiful world. He fell and to this day is unredeemed and so he suffers the miseries of his unredeemed state and will continue to suffer until the Messiah comes to save him, or at least a Messianic Age, which we confidently expect. The coming of the Messianic Age, if not the Messiah, will be mediated by the Jews, who are a light unto the nations and with whom God entered into a unique covenant.

(e) (*Baptist speaking*) C3. Man is saved. He suffered the Fall, was promised a savior from the Jews. A savior came, Jesus Christ, to save us from sin and misery and death. The Good News of his coming was broadcast to the ends of the earth for all men to hear and be baptized and saved. The Kingdom of God exists here and now and we are in it. We have freed ourselves from the Catholic Church and other idolatries. I have had a personal encounter with my Lord and Savior Jesus Christ and I am saved once and for all and live now and forever in a state of blessedness, now on this earth and forever in heaven.

(f) Other (specify).

(CHECK ONE)

Thought Experiment: Sexuality and space travel.

As project designer at NASA, you must select a two-person crew to undertake a prolonged mission. Their objective: to act as emissaries to a civilization with whom communication is already established. It is a vital mission. They are more advanced than we. We, with an estimated 40 percent chance of survival, need their wisdom as well as their technology. Their goodwill is our objective. Your task, therefore, is to select the best, most admirable specimens of *Homo sapiens sapiens.*

It is also your responsibility to provide for the human needs of the astronauts. In the objective scientific stance so characteristic of the twentieth and twenty-first centuries, sexual needs are viewed as but one of the many human needs which must be provided for within the cramped confines of the spaceship, e.g., need for food, water, oxygen, exercise, simulated gravity, and so on. Previous missions have shown that pornography, *Penthouse* magazine, tapes of Nancy Friday, inflatable female dolls, and masturbation have been unsatisfactory sexual outlets. Nor have inhibitory hormones, saltpeter, cold baths worked.

You conclude that human sexual needs require humans to satisfy them.

It was decided against sending a husband and wife, not merely for the reason that a husband-and-wife team was not available, but because of evidence adduced by staff social scientists that the institution of marriage had fallen on such evil days that four out of five married couples studied—as well as unmarried live-in couples—were already so sick of each other that no one would take responsibility for what they might do to each other after years in space.

Accordingly, you have five crews available from whom you must choose one.

(1) A pair of good-humored and well-qualified astronauts, a man and a woman, who have no religious scruples and no marital or emotional attachments, a Burt Reynolds and a Shirley MacLaine type, each highly skilled technically, each sexually experienced and happily and actively and somewhat casually heterosexual, and who, though not well known to each other, find each other attractive—but who, let us admit it, are a little dumb and know next to nothing of Western civilization, literature, or history, beyond last year's winner of the Superbowl and the comparative ratings of Snyder, Carson, and Letterman during the last ratings sweeps.

(2) A pair of lesbians, an inseparable couple, pleasant, fastidious, housekeeping, "married" middle-aged homebodies with a low sex drive and a high toleration for closeness and intimacy. Besides being excellent astronauts, both are highly cultivated. One is by avocation a historian, the other a poet.

(3) A pair of male homosexuals from San Francisco. Strangers to each other before training, promiscuous as chimpanzees, they find each other attractive. Outside their technical proficiency, they have a range of interests; one was active in San Francisco politics, the other a Rhodes Scholar in medieval studies.

(4) A lapsed Catholic, Irish, Midwestern male chauvinist, and a militantly feminist woman. Despite, or perhaps because of, their differences, they get along famously. The male is perhaps the best qualified technically of the lot, his marriage is on the rocks, and he is highly sexed, humorous, and salacious as only a Christian or ex-Christian can be (as horny as a preacher, as the saying goes). The female is a handsome Gloria Steinem–Radcliffe type who subscribes to the NASA view that sexual drives and needs are normal biological properties of the human organism, and is willing to satisfy hers and his on the basis of an equality between the sexes—i.e., it must be understood that she is as free as he to initiate sexual behavior. (Her insistence on this point at the first interview made the male astronaut's eyes sparkle with anticipation.)

These two were technically the best qualified of the crews, but one thing troubled the NASA project manager. In the standard questionnaire, the male astronaut responded to questions 45, 46, and 47 in the following fashion:

Q.: Do you now or have you ever professed a religion?
A.: Yes. But not now.

Q.: What was it?

A.: Catholic.

Q.: Do you regard sexual intercourse outside marriage as sinful?

A.: Technically, at the most. But in the interests of God and country I will make the sacrifice.

What bothered NASA was not that he might be compromising his principles—indeed, he seemed gleeful at the prospect—but rather a certain irony and flippancy in his answer. Beware of smart-ass ironical types, warned one of the older astronauts, the last of the line of un-ironical men beginning with John Glenn and Neal Armstrong. The NASA psychologist noted that the irony might conceal a deeply rooted scruple which might surface later in the mission. One thing the mission didn't need was a guilty astronaut. Imagine an adulterous and penitent Catholic looking for a priest and a confessional on PC3 like a character in a Graham Greene novel.

(5) Two Nobel Laureates, both male and past middle age, who, though just barely competent as astronauts, expressed a willingness in the interests of humanity to masturbate regularly during the ten years of a mission, saving and freezing the ejaculate for the insemination of millions of suitable if intellectually inferior women toward the end of upgrading the human gene pool.

Which crew would you choose? State your reasons.

(CHECK ONE)

A SPACE ODYSSEY
(II)

(20) THE SELF MAROONED IN THE COSMOS: *What do you do if there is no man Friday out there and we really are alone?*

A starship is returning to earth after a voyage of eighteen years[*]

It set out with hope and excitement and good reason to expect success.

After many years of fruitless monitoring of radio emissions from space, the spectrum analyzer at SETI picked up a patterned transmission in the 1400-megahertz range which could not, apparently, be accounted for by the random noise of the Cosmos. The source was the region of Barnard's Star some six light-years distant. There were bursts of energy with a lesser radiation in between. The configuration was repeated over and over again. Some of the clusters could be counted as prime numbers. Very possibly it was a message in a nested code: a kind of palimpsest consisting of an overlay of prime numbers (but somewhat garbled) to make contact, and under it a primer to establish a language, and under that, the message.

Hopes were raised further by an analysis of a perturbation of Barnard's Star suggesting an orbiting planet, perhaps two, and now confirmed with such a high degree of accuracy that only two planets approximately the size of the earth could cause it.

---

[*] The adventures recounted here owe something to Walter M. Miller's extraordinary novel, *A Canticle for Liebowitz*, from which I have borrowed Liebowitz and the state of Utah.

But the message, if it was a message, could not be decoded. No doubt it was garbled by some intervening source of radiation.

Finally, it was decided at NASA to send a manned vehicle, the Bussard interstellar ramjet, which accelerates to velocities approaching the speed of light by means of a frontal scoop that funnels hydrogen atoms into a fusion engine and ejects them through a rear jet.

Some extraordinary considerations went into the planning. One was the generally accepted, though not yet proved, consequence of Einstein's general theory, namely that—and here the mind boggled—though the voyagers on the starship would experience time as a lapse of eighteen years and would be eighteen years older when they returned, between 400 and 500 years would have elapsed on earth upon the return of the starship—depending on how close to the speed of light the Bussard ramjet could drive the ship.

The human problems were unprecedented. Friends and family of the crew, and fellow scientists, would be as long dead to them as Galileo and Columbus are to us. A crew must be found who shared the following unusual characteristics: they must be willing and able to live together in close quarters for eighteen years; they must be willing to leave behind family, husbands, wives, forever; they must be prepared to return to an earth which would either be destroyed or so technologically advanced that their homecoming in the ancient ramjet would be something like Rip Van Winkle riding a mule into the Jet Propulsion Lab in Pasadena. Finally, in the event of the former, they must reproduce themselves.

The first problem was approached by calling for volunteers who for their own good and sufficient reasons were willing to leave—perhaps, as in at least one case, for patriotic reasons: somebody has to do it, we're in trouble, and maybe the civilization on Barnard P1 can help us. Or for less admirable though just as compelling reasons: wanting out, bad marriages, wanderlust in the old U.S. head-for-the-territory, walk-out-the-front-door-and-hit-the-road tradition, or just being sick and tired of the old earth with its sad past and sadder prospects for the future, sick and tired of living in the gloomy condos of Houston, Pasadena, and Canaveral. Whatever. Volunteers were not hard to come by. NASA was deluged by thousands of applicants, not merely nuts, but qualified scientists. Apparently, many people wanted out. The main problem was not the choice of individual crew members but rather the social composition of the crew. After a careful review of cultural trends, such as the breakdown of monogamous marriage and the newest experiences in communal living, open marriage, serial monogamy, polygamy, and in the light of recent discoveries of genetic differences in the right- and left-brain cortices of men and women, a crew of four was hit upon. One man and three women. Consultation with the best American neurologists and behaviorist psychologists and group-psychotherapists and with the most highly regarded Moslem sociologists and neo-Mormon marriage counselors confirmed the decision. The projected life style was to be called "programmed serial monogamy."

Different social combinations had proved disastrous in simulated environments. Two couples or a triangle, one man and two women, or one woman and two men, failed to tolerate a year's confinement. A single couple, married or not, either fell to murderous quarreling or became so bored with each other that performance fell off. In the case of two couples, it generally happened that one couple fell out and the spouse of one sex took up with the spouse of the opposite sex in the second couple. But it did not generally happen that the leftover pair bonded. There seldom occurred a symmetrical swap. Triangles were always disrupted by destructive pair-bonding. Somebody got left out and either sulked or became violent.

One-man–three-women teams seemed to get along best. In a post-Christian and post-feminist era, it appeared that women generally accept a polygamous relationship, given a reasonable respect for their persons and professional skills, while men were at the least less bored and at the most quite pleased. Women, it seemed, were different from men after all, not worse or better, but different. In the event of pair-bonding between man and woman, the two surplus women seemed content with a relationship, not necessarily homosexual, with each other. The sole man was enjoined, however, to treat all three women with loving and impartial care insofar as he was able. The men in the sealed-environment experiments readily agreed and by and large succeeded.

The captain was a native of Rye, New York, of Dutch descent, and named after a Roman emperor: Marcus Aurelius Schuyler. Thirty-two years old, once a history major at Harvard, he changed course, graduated from the Air Force Academy, and went to M.I.T. for astronomy. A somewhat wayward, wintry, and sardonic man, as wintry as his name-sake—he was the sort who could sit in Robinson Hall listening to a lecture on the Battle of Verdun, gaze out the window at the tender green of the spring trees, suddenly reach a decision, close his book, and walk away forever, head for Colorado to fly. His consciousness was reflected and folded in upon itself. Though he might appear as stolid and as steady as one of the old astronauts or a commercial airline pilot—even a little dumb—in fact he was very much conscious of doing just that: playing the unflappable captain. It was his complex way to make the untoward odd decision and to take pleasure both in savoring the very oddness of it and in sticking to it. For example, after the launch of the shuttle to the orbital platform from which he would depart in the starship Copernicus 4, the shuttle crossed the Northeast coastline some hundred miles up and rising. Looking down through the clouds, he could just make out Long Island nuzzling into the continent like a great whale. There, just off its nose and in a sheltered cove, his thirty-foot ketch *Andrea*, he knew, was bobbing gently at her mooring. His pleasure came from *not* looking down again and in *not* thinking that he would never see it, the boat *Andrea*, or her, the woman Andrea, again.

Why did he volunteer for the mission? Because it was both the odd and the necessary thing to do and the pleasure came from it being both. Though he took as dark a view of the human condition as the Emperor, like the Emperor he also took his pleasure in acting well even though he knew it probably would not avail and that things would end badly. Like the early-twentieth-century psychologist Freud, he believed that there is no end to the mischief and hatred which men harbor deep in themselves and unknown to themselves and no end to their capacity to deceive themselves and that though they loved life, they probably loved death more and in the end *thanatos* would likely win over *eros*. He and his fellowmen, he knew, loved themselves and war too well and nothing short of a miracle would save them and he did not believe in miracles. But he volunteered nonetheless, or rather because he didn't believe. He was like a Christian who had lost his faith in everything but the Fall of man. In another time he might have said that earthlings were like the Gadarene swine, who were possessed by demons and were rushing headlong to destruction.

So why not try for Barnard's Star's planet for this very reason, that even if there were an ETI there, he could not imagine what it could tell a human that would help the earth four hundred years from now?

Neither the captain nor his superiors were hopeful about the earth's prospects. Indeed, he had been given secret orders that in the event of a catastrophe on earth during his voyage, he had permission either to request sanctuary on Barnard's Star's planet or to colonize it. Surely, one man and three young women had at least as good a chance of starting a new race as Adam and Eve.

And why was he chosen from the thousands of volunteers? Perhaps because of the very complexity and reflectedness of his character: that he knew how to perform as coolly as the most stolid astronaut, and had also this odd "humanistic" background, a history major who specialized in the old twentieth century. So, with only the vaguest notion that somehow a scientist and pilot with a "humanistic" background might somehow be able to get along with three women for eighteen years—or for the next fifty years—and with an intelligent being on Barnard P1, NASA chose him. His father being Governor of New York didn't hurt him either.

The crew members were:

Tiffany, a tall blond astrophysicist-psychotherapist, from Cal Tech, age 27. In her vita she listed as her hobbies: cross-country skiing, wok cooking, "giving and receiving strokes in a creative stroke field."

Kimberly, a petite brunette linguist-semioticist from Bloomington, Indiana, age 22, the youngest but also the best and the brightest in her field, who, if anyone could, could decipher the code from the ETI on Barnard P1. She liked, besides semiotics: walking in the autumn woods, reading the Vedas in the original Sanskrit, gazing into firelight with a kindred spirit.

The third crew member was the medical officer, Dr. Jane Smith of Nashville, age 23. The oddity about her was that she had been married, listed no hobbies, and put herself down as a Methodist. Hers was old Tennessee Scotch-Irish stock. "You must be the last Methodist in Tennessee," said the Captain, thinking to make a pleasantry. Her smile was thin. The rumor was that, competent though she was, and brilliant though her contributions to hypothermic hibernation were, her "religious preference" had not hurt her with NASA. The Christian minority was as loud as it was small, as shrill as it was shrinking. Affirmative action for minorities in the space program had been sustained by the Supreme Court. The last mission to Pluto had been manned by a black and Hispanic crew who had not been heard from. Some bad jokes were told. So the present mission was manned by three women and one WASPP (White Anglo-Saxon Post-Protestant) male. Jane Smith had graduated from Vanderbilt, taken her residency in aerospace medicine, and contributed valuable papers on hypothermic hibernation techniques. Her discovery was that both the tissue damage and the discomfort (excruciating pain, if the truth be known) of the hibernation cycle could be minimized by the injection of an endomorph (already known as the Smith-Bowers endomorph). Indeed, the usual cramps and bends of the thaw were replaced by a mild euphoria, as if one had awakened from a pleasant dream. ("You look just like Scarlett O'Hara waking up," said the Captain, a student of old twentieth-century culture, to Kimberly the first time she came out of the deep freeze.)

In a word, the Captain suspected Jane might have exaggerated her Methodism in her application, for had she not also signed the "sexual access" form?—that is, the consent agreement by which she contracted to make herself, "her person," available for "the biological and social objectives" of the mission, which objectives also included "the emotional needs" of her fellow crew members. (Let it be added quickly that the Captain had to sign the same contract. This was no seraglio.)

The shifts were arranged so that the Captain took his watches with successive partners or second officers. The shifts were of six months' duration: two astronauts in hibernation, the other two "awake," that is, alternating eight-hour watches, with an hour or so overlap to allow for scientific experiments and whatever social interaction or "stroke field" might seem appropriate. Thus, in a three-year period, each crew member would have spent six months "awake" with each other crew member.

Then there were the "simul-dehibes"—that is, periods of simultaneous dehibernation when all four crew members were "awake" for a period of one month annually, at which time the progress of the mission could be assessed, scientific and group-interaction experiments performed, and just plain socializing could take place, e.g., bridge, Scrabble, Monopoly, books read aloud, playlets performed, video-stereo-hologram tapes played, dancing in place. For a while, earth TV could be watched, for about a month into the mission—but as the ramjet accelerated, the TV action slowed in a Doppler effect, so that in old reruns of M*A*S*H, a favorite, Hawkeye and the nurses spoke in ever lower and more sepulchral tones and moved like dream figures walking in glue.

An open and free sexuality was programmed, based on Prescott's statistical analysis of pre-industrial societies and his conclusion that, in those societies in which sexual activity and the pleasures of the body are not repressed, theft, violence, war, and religion are minimal. Whereas, in those societies in which infants are disciplined and adults are inhibited, there tends to be a high incidence of murder, war, and belief in a supernatural being. Hugging and touch were encouraged even during routine scientific experiments.

The starship was therefore equipped with a nursery. The project planners had two goals in mind: one, to devise a mini-society in which affection was lavished freely between adults and upon children; and two: just in case *Homo sapiens sapiens* had been destroyed on earth, then at least a tiny remnant would have survived, either as refugees on Barnard P1 or as colonists elsewhere, or perhaps even to return to earth.

The worst case: the earth five hundred years later, blasted and depopulated but perhaps habitable, and Copernicus 4 returning, limping home with four middle-aged astronauts and x number of children ranging from one to seventeen years old.

Even in the worst case, life might not only survive but prevail and multiply and once again fill the earth, with a new variety of *Homo sapiens sapiens*, an affectionate, hugging, promiscuous, peaceful breed. (Genetic inbreeding was something to worry about, but the most exhaustive genetic studies of the four ruled out all known pathogenic genes.)

SCENE: Three days after launch from orbital platform and one week before the first hibernation.

The crew: taking their ease for the first time since the rigors of launch, instrument check, adjusting the hydrogen scoop, counting hydrogen atoms, calibrating the engine. The steady Bussard acceleration is mild, scarcely more noticeable than the slight heavy-footedness one feels in a swift elevator.

It was like moving into a new house. Furniture is placed, beds are made, the kitchen stocked, and the folks sit down in the living room, exhausted but relaxed, to have a look around, to savor their new dwelling.

The four are sitting at their consoles in the command module. It is hardly larger than a big bathroom. From the command module a good-sized tube, not unlike the tunnel in the old B-52, leads aft to rec-room-gym, to hibe units (which look like Sears' Best freezers) and bedrooms (smaller than an Amtrak roomette: here intimacy need not be encouraged, it is obligatory), nursery and supply rooms, and finally the engine.

The four chairs in command are comfortable, can tilt, vibrate, or swivel to face each other or the computer displays.

For some reason, no one looks directly at anyone else—except Jane Smith, who—perhaps because she is flight surgeon—gazes curiously from one to the other:

Tiffany: sprawled, long-legged and handsome in her jumpsuit, yawns and stretches more perhaps than she needs to.

Kimberly: frowning, preoccupied, a book open in her lap (volume 15 of *The Complete Works of B. F. Skinner*), chewing on a fingernail for all the world as if she were sitting in the library of the University of Indiana.

Jane Smith: watching them, taking note of the angle at which the chairs are swiveled and toward whom, which leg is crossed, etc. She is smiling slightly. She and the Captain have the first six-month watch—that is, they will alternate eight-hour watches for six months while the other two hibernate.

Notice the Captain.

He is every inch the professional, lounging at his ease the way a professional does after doing his thing and doing it well, a bit weary after the hundreds of items on the checklist, after cranking up the ramjet, a bit red-eyed and unshaven, eyes half-closed, rocking just enough in his chair to flex his neck while he massages it gently. But wait. Is he as simple as that? You would perhaps notice, as Jane Smith does (that is why she is smiling) that he is complex and somewhat folded upon himself. Which is to say not only that he is lounging at his ease, which is what one would expect, but that he is quite conscious of doing so and of how he does it. Would he be lounging in quite the same way, massaging his neck in quite the same way, if the women were not present? Indeed, he is first-rate at his job, but he is also something like jetliner Captain Dean Martin in an *Airport* movie who has just made a successful landing of a disabled 747—while three stewardesses watch. That, too, is a pleasure for Deano the actor sitting in his mock-up jet. But Captain Schuyler has the best of both worlds: he is a real pilot but he is also a good actor, which is to say he knows how to do what he does and also how to do it with an actor's calculated effect. He is aware of his effect on the women.

Accelerating toward the speed of light as he exits his world, he was never more successfully and triumphantly in his world.

The eyes are important. The women make a point of watching him while not appearing to, except Jane Smith. He makes a point of not watching them, while appearing watchable.

Can it be said of him what the Apostle John wrote in his first letter, that he had the best of this world even as he left it, the pride of life and the lust of the eyes?

Hardly, not lust exactly, in the current meaning, but lust rather in the Old English sense of *lysten*, to please or take delight. Because lust is a craving and *lysten* is a taking and giving of delight. Delight in the three women. He wished to delight them in return. A twofold delight in playing out the role of Captain, doing his job, and lounging at his ease, and the added aesthetic delight of consciously doing so in the way the women would expect, and so as a preliminary stratagem, a male display, in what would surely be a complex courtship.

The stratagem is partially successful. It "works" with Tiffany and Kimberly in the way it is calculated to, just as the sight of weary Deano, collar unbuttoned, tie loosened, massaging his neck in the 747, worked with the stewardesses. In this case, "working" means that they are attracted to him for reasons which he knows about but they don't. But it doesn't work with Jane Smith because she knows what he is doing: hence the ironic smile through her eyes. But wait. Does it not work for this very reason? That he knows that his little ruse will not succeed with her and that she will know

that he knows that it won't. At any rate, the encounter between the Captain and Dr. Jane Smith is of a different order
of complexity.

Years pass. Kimberly and Tiffany were impregnated three
times outward bound. Dr. Jane Smith refused sex on the first
watch with the Captain. Her excuse: Somebody has to run
the nursery. Her second excuse: We're not married. Her
third excuse: I'm married to someone else.

THE CAPTAIN: But we're a year into the flight. Your hus-
band is 123 years old, or dead.
DR. JANE SMITH: We can't be sure.
THE CAPTAIN: But you signed the sexual access form.
DR. JANE SMITH: I lied.
THE CAPTAIN: Don't you like me?
DR. JANE SMITH: Very much.
THE CAPTAIN: I like you very much. More than the others.
DR. JANE SMITH: I know—though you seem to like them
well enough.
THE CAPTAIN: Good God. You're jealous.
DR. JANE SMITH: Yes.
THE CAPTAIN: This is the first day of our second six-month
watch together. Are we going to do crosswords and Great
Books again? I love you.
DR. JANE SMITH: I know. Marry me.
THE CAPTAIN: Marry you! Why? How?
DR. JANE SMITH: You're the captain. The captain of a ship
can—
THE CAPTAIN: The captain of a ship cannot marry himself.
DR. JANE SMITH: Who says? You stand there, say the
words, then move over here, give the response.
THE CAPTAIN: What words? I don't have the book.

DR. JANE SMITH: I do.

THE CAPTAIN: Good Lord. What about the others?

DR. JANE SMITH: Don't tell them.

So they were married. Dr. Jane Smith conceived and delivered herself of a son. She baptized him, not by pouring, sprinkling, or immersion—what with zero gravity—but with a squirt from the drinking tube.

The names of the first seven children were Krishna, Vishnu, Indira (out of Kimberly), Anna Freud, Oppie, Irene-Curie (out of Tiffany), and John (out of Dr. Jane Smith).

The "message" from Barnard's Star turned out to be a false alarm, a non-message. It was no more than an interference effect from the powerful magnetic fields of the two Barnard planets, producing a complex pulsar transmission in the radio frequencies—much like two metronomes set at different speeds. Thus, where a single pulsar would go tick-tick-tick, this "message" went something like tock-tick-tock-tick-tick-tick-tock, a non-message fiendishly close to a message.

Barnard's two planets were dead. They were also without oxygen or water and hence not colonizable.

More ominous than the bad news from Barnard was the bad news from home. Even as the ramjet approached the speed of light, it should have been overtaken by a few messages from earth. But after five years starship time—ninety years earth time—the messages ceased altogether.

Nevertheless, the crew took comfort. Any number of technical things could have gone wrong. After the disappointment at Barnard, everyone secretly looked forward to the return voyage after the great swing around the star when they should be running into a regular blizzard of outgoing messages from earth.

But earth was silent. Even after repeated queries: *JPL, do you read? Do you read? Respond on any or all of designated frequencies*—and even after five years of allowing for responses: silence.

Everyone knew what had happened. The Richardson survey, from his *The Statistics of Deadly Quarrels*, had proved all too reliable. The only unknown quantity was the magnitude of the final war. Was it an M10—the end of human life on the planet? an M9? an M5?

The long voyage home was like a dream. Five more children were born: Carl Jung out of Tiffany, Siddhartha and Chomsky out of Kimberly, Sarah and Mary Ann out of Dr. Jane Smith.

Other than the begetting, the care and feeding of infants, the education of children and teens, the adults were mostly silent—silent, until, as the starship neared earth, there came the inevitable speculation:

How bad is it? or was it? Even if it were an M10, 90 percent of the Cesium 137 radiation would have decayed after a hundred years. But the nitrogen in the upper atmosphere would have been oxidized, destroying significant amounts of ozone. The resulting solar ultraviolet effect would last for years. Birds would go blind—blind birds can't find insects and so they die. Blind bees can't pollinate plants. Would it be an earth swarming with locusts, seas teeming with blind fish? Even if there were survivors, how many would develop skin cancers? All the light-skinned? How would crops and microorganisms be affected?

But the favorite, the endless, the obsessive speculation of which they never tired:

Where will you go? What will you do? What about the children?

There was only one agreement. After eighteen years of

living together in a space the size of a 727 fuselage, they were all thoroughly sick of each other and wanted to go their separate ways. With two exceptions.

THE CAPTAIN: Where do you want to go?

TIFFANY: I'm going to the coast of Oregon, where I once spent the summer doing anthropology with an Indian tribe. They were fishermen. They lived well and simply. It should be the safest spot in the U.S. from fallout. And the fish are least likely to be contaminated by radiation or ultraviolet.

KIMBERLY: I want to go to Uxmal in the Yucatan. I have an idea about deciphering the glyphs. I lived there once in a pyramid next to a lovely deep cenote. I have a feeling that if anything has survived, it has.

THE CAPTAIN: What about your kids?

TIFFANY-AND-KIMBERLY: Oh, they all think they're Jane's anyhow.

THE CAPTAIN: What about you, Jane? Where do you want to go?

DR. JANE SMITH: Lost Cove, Tennessee. I was born there. It's a tiny valley of the Cumberland plateau sealed off by a ridge. No roads, no phones, no TV. Only three farms and a cave. Good water, sweet white corn, quail, squirrel, deer, fish, wild pig. I haven't had pork sausage, grits, and collards in twenty years. All projections of East–West fallout patterns missed it. I think I'll take my chances.

THE CAPTAIN: Would you take the children?

DR. JANE SMITH: Sure. Can you fly us there?

THE CAPTAIN: Yes, but we have to land in Utah first.

DR. JANE SMITH: What will you do, Captain?

THE CAPTAIN: (Why didn't she invite me to come with her to Tennessee?) I'm going back to Long Island. I don't care what they've done to it. I'm getting in my ketch and sailing to Montauk.

DR. JANE SMITH (*shyly*): Wouldn't you rather come with
me to Tennessee?
THE CAPTAIN: Yes.

The starship made two low orbits before landing at Bonneville: the first fly-by to see the Eastern Hemisphere by night;
the second, the Western. Silently, like Lucifer in starlight,
leaning on his great wings, they flew low over the dark
northern continents.

London was dark. Europe was dark. Moscow was dark.
China was dark. Japan was dark. San Francisco was dark.
Chicago was dark. New York was dark.

At dawn on April 12, eighteen years after launch in starship time, 457 years in earth time, the starship Copernicus 4
set down on schedule on the salt flats at Bonneville, Utah,
the Captain landing at 190 knots as easily as an ancient airline
pilot landing a 727. One does not forget how to ride a bicycle,
swim, or fly an airplane.

After a long silence, the Captain requested an external
radiation reading from Kimberly. Negative.

There was no one and nothing to be seen except the rusty
shards of old steel maintenance sheds from the twenty-first
century.

They stepped out into the sweet, heavy desert air. The
problem was walking—but not for the children! Perhaps
they were like the newborn of the Arctic tern who fly to the
Dry Tortugas, never having been there before, yet land and
know it for home.

Despite Dr. Jane Smith's careful program of exercise and
calcium maintenance, the adults were limber-legged as sailors
and blind as bats in the dazzling Utah sun.

The children ran and fell and jumped and fell like the
Beatles on a soccer field.

They made for the nearest shade and the nearest shelter—of all things, the ruins of a rest stop on old Interstate 80 between Salt Lake City and San Francisco.

They sat at a picnic table, the returning earthlings, speechless and bemused. The rusting hulks of ancient eighteen-wheelers, Airstreams, and twenty-first-century camper-choppers (helicopters-with-tents) littered the parking area. Close by, the broken concrete of old I-80 was drifted by salt and sand like a Roman road in Cyrenaica. But a single aspen shaded them, its crisp new leaves shivering and glittering like new money in the rising sun. A single buzzard wheeled high in the sky. As they watched, a green lizard crawled on the table, elbows sprung, cocked an eye at them, and inflated a red bladder.

The earth was alive.

There were also human survivors. And an odd lot they were, the four who rescued the stranded astronauts.

One was Aristarchus Jones, an astronomer who lived in the old SAC headquarters under a mountain at Colorado Springs.

The other three were Benedictine monks from a nearby abbey where Jones had been living for a month.

What was he, Jones, doing here? Why, he had come to meet them. They were expected. Or rather, Jones had years ago come into possession of some documents from the old JPL in Pasadena and had made the calculation that if Copernicus 4 had failed to colonize Barnard's P1, it would return to earth—ETA: some time in April of this year.

So here he was. In February he had ridden a horse out old I-80 from Denver, taking two weeks, and had been put up by the Benedictines while he searched the skies for Copernicus 4.

The Benedictines? They were even odder. The three were

all that remained, the remnant of a thriving community which
at its peak, a period of religious rivival after the second of
the great wars of the twentieth century, had as many as three
hundred men.

Now there were three: the abbot, a dried-up old sourdough
with a wisp of a beard and a nose like a buzzard's beak, and
a running sore on his forehead; and two black monks, not
"black monks" as all black-robed Benedictines used to be
called, but black men, Negroes in the old usage, who were
monks. Four white monks had died within the decade, of
assorted cancers. Black men, it seemed, had the skin melanin
to withstand the noxious ultraviolet.

The community had managed to survive, if this odd trio
could be called a community, thanks to the prescience of an
abbot of the twenty-first century who had foreseen WWIII
of the year 2069 and had excavated a huge shelter in the
sandstone under the abbey deep enough and well-stocked
enough to survive the hundred-year decay time of Cesium 137.

The eighteen astronauts, young and old—the youngest,
Sarah, a babe in arms, in the arms of Dr. Jane Smith—took
their ease in the monastery garden next to an undistinguished
barracks-like church and cloister built of twentieth-century
cinder blocks, ugly but durable. The children watched in
astonishment as the monks walked in tiny procession, bearing
aloft fronds of a desert plant. It was Palm Sunday.

There were also children at the abbey, a dozen or so,
mostly genetically malformed and misbegotten: retardates,
dolichocephalics ("steeple-heads"), bilateral cleft palates
("wolf-snouts"), armless, legless, depigmented, multipig-
mented ("harlequins")—yet a remarkably cheerful and playful lot.

The two groups eyed each other. The first, the earthlings,
looking more like visitors from space than the visitors from
space: three monks in black, and Aristarchus Jones, a young

blond Californian who wore a loose white garment fitted with a hood with eyeholes which protected him from the ultraviolet but made him look like a Ku Kluxer from olden time.

Abbot Liebowitz, ex-physicist, ex-Brooklynite, looked like a shtetl shopkeeper stranded in the Sinai desert for forty years.

The two black monks looked like Amos 'n' Andy, one small and sober and smart as Sidney Poitier; the other ponderous, windy, and funny.

The Captain had some questions, while the space children, who after a week had got the hang of earth, climbed trees, pulled grass, shied rocks as if they'd been born to it. They, the space children, after their initial astonishment, got along fine with the "misbegotten," learned baseball from them, took them aboard Copernicus 4, taught them video-computer games.

THE CAPTAIN: What was it, an M7?

ABBOT: The old war? An M9, I'm afraid.

THE CAPTAIN: How many are left?

JONES AND ABBOT (*looking at each other*): You mean people?

THE CAPTAIN: Yes.

JONES: We don't know. Not enough.

THE CAPTAIN: Not enough for what?

JONES: To sustain civilization.

THE CAPTAIN: Well, who do you know for a fact to have survived?

JONES: A couple of thousand in California. Six in Colorado Springs.

THE CAPTAIN: New York?

ABBOT: Don't know. The last courier on his way to the West Coast said there were a hundred or so on Long Island.

THE CAPTAIN (*to Abbot*): What about Asia? Europe?

Don't you have communication with other monasteries? Churches?

ABBOT (*shrugging*): Don't know about Europe. A few Catholics here and there in North America, a few churches, but no bishops.

THE CAPTAIN: The Pope?

ABBOT: Don't know.

DR. JANE SMITH: Any Methodists?

ABBOT: Very few Methodists.

DR. JANE SMITH (*eyeing him*): Jews?

ABBOT (*reviving*): Yeah. A young Israeli came through here several years ago looking for his family in San Francisco. He had made a boat and sailed from Tyre, all alone. He said there were several hundred Israelis holed up in the caves of Qumran.

THE CAPTAIN: To get away from the radiation?

ABBOT: No, to get away from the Arabs.

THE CAPTAIN: Are they still fighting?

ABBOT: Yes. But radiation is no longer a danger. Cesium 137 radiation became minimal a hundred years ago.

THE CAPTAIN: Then why hasn't the species replenished or begun to replenish? Or has it?

ABBOT AND JONES *look at each other*.

JONES: There's another problem.

THE CAPTAIN: What?

JONES: Sterility.

THE CAPTAIN: From the Cesium? How could that be? Your parents were not sterile. The lizards and buzzards are not sterile.

JONES: We don't really know. Maybe a cumulative effect of Cesium in the food chain. Maybe the ultraviolet, maybe a delayed effect of the chemical warfare. Anyhow, it has been slowly progressive until now—

THE CAPTAIN: Now what?

ABBOT: Now we estimate an incidence of 98 percent sterility in humans. There has not been a recorded birth in Utah, Colorado, or California in more than a year.

THE CAPTAIN (*looking at Jones*): And you?

JONES: Viable sperm count: zero.

THE CAPTAIN (*looking at monks, thinks better of it, looks at Jones*): You married?

JONES (*looking at Tiffany, another blond Californian*): No.

MONK AMOS (*solemn and a bit platitudinous, like Amos in Amos 'n' Andy*): It's tragic to see people want children and not be able to have them. What a joy to see these children!

THE CAPTAIN: How about the sexual drive? Is that affected, too, in some people?

MONK ANDY: In very few white folks and no niggers at all.

THE CAPTAIN: Let me get this straight. What you're saying is that you're probably the last generation on earth.

JONES: If not this, then the next is the last, surely.

ABBOT (*brightening*): Until you came along.

THE CAPTAIN (*after a long pause*): Do you have a plan?

ABBOT AND JONES: We have two plans. Two irreconcilable plans. Each involves you. I'm afraid you're going to have to decide.

THE CAPTAIN: Let's hear them.

Dr. Aristarchus Jones's Proposal

Here are the facts:

The human species is finished on earth. Due to the delayed and cumulative effect of Ce 137 radiation or the reduction of ozone in the atmosphere by nitrous oxides and the resulting ultraviolet flare, male sterility is approaching 100 percent, and female is not far behind. In a word, we are either the last generation on earth or the next to last. You, Captain, and your crew are obviously fertile, but it is problematical how long you will remain so—a year? a month? And do you imagine that when your children mature sexually, they will be fertile?

My proposal: that we colonize Europa, one of the Galilean satellites of Jupiter. You, Captain, made a fly-by eighteen years ago and know better than I that it is probably habitable: planet-size, covered by water ice, evidence of newly emerging land—the famous greening seen nowhere else but here on earth—no vulcanism, no impact craters, what appears to be a river system and, most important of all, an atmosphere of 10 percent oxygen.

Your starship has sufficient reactor fuel for launch and to attain sufficient ramjet speeds to activate the hydrogen scoop. Hence, a journey of weeks.

Here in the good monks' cellar I have found a supply of seeds, algae, plants, small mammals, and even insects. I have books, music, Shakespeare on cassettes.

As a matter of fact, we have no choice except to stay here and die. I will go along—you will need me as a technical adviser. Moreover, Tiffany and I already have a relationship. Who knows, I may not be totally sterile—no one ever is 100 percent. After all, it only takes one spermatozoon.

With a bit of luck, we can colonize Europa in much the same way as Europe colonized the New World, *except that*— and here is the exciting part!—there is no reason why we cannot develop a society such as the one my namesake lived in in ancient Ionia, a society based on reason and science, and do so without repeating the mistakes of the past, for example, the Dark Ages, two thousand years of Plato and Judaism and Christianity—a sexually free and peace-loving society where the sciences and arts can flourish freed from the superstitions and repressions of religion—no offense to the good monks, who are in fact invited to come along. I think it appropriate, with your permission, to change the name of Europa to New Ionia. At long last, we are going to put behind us forever the interminable quarrels of the people of the Book—first the Jews, then the Christians, then Islam. There will be no Middle East on Ionia, no Christian *vs.* Jew, no Christian *vs.* Moslem, Shi-ite *vs.* Sunnite, Moslem *vs.* Jew, Protestant *vs.* Catholic.

There is no reason why we cannot start a new society on another planet just as we started a new society in the New World.

In fact, we have no choice. Europa lives. This planet is dying.

There is no time to lose. I calculate that the launch window for Europa will occur for only a few days next month.

That is my proposal.

ABBOT: Are the children invited?

ARISTARCHUS: The space children are. It would make no sense to perpetuate genetic defects.

ABBOT: I see.

Abbot Liebowitz's Proposal

Here are the facts:

The human species may or may not be finished on earth. Perhaps the incidence of sterility is lower in Seattle or New Zealand. We do not know.

But it makes no difference. In either case, I could not go. Why not?

Because I believe that God exists and that he created the Cosmos (the Big Bang, as you vulgarly call it, embarrasses you, Aristarchus, doesn't it?), that he created man through evolution, in the latest moment of which, perhaps the last Ice Age, man became ensouled and came to himself as man, body and spirit; that God thus created man as a person who had gifts of knowledge and love but most of all of freedom, that he somehow encountered a catastrophe, God alone knows what, used his freedom badly, and chose badly—perhaps chose himSELF, the one thing he can never know of itself, rather than God—and has been in trouble ever since. That, as a consequence, God himself intervened in the history of this insignificant planet, through a covenant with an even more obscure tribe, the Jews, through his son, a Jew who actually lived as a man on this earth, him and no other, through founding a church, the Catholic Church based on a very mediocre, intemperate Catholic, Peter, also a Jew; that he, God, is somehow inextricably and permanently, even hopelessly, involved with the two, the Jews and the Catholic Church, until the end of earth time.

In a sense, nothing has changed. Here is the Christian remnant, still hanging on, a slightly mad enclave of odd sorts, gentile-bums collected from the hedgerows and invited to the feast. And over there in Israel, we know, is still the Jewish remnant, still hanging on, long ago dispersed and now come back to the same place, proud and stiff-necked as ever, still persecuted, still fighting Assyrians. What has changed?

I am both. I am both Jew and Catholic, whether Jew or Catholic like it or not, and generally they do not, usually have no use for each other, in fact, and even less use for me. The Jews think I have apostasized, and the Catholics think I am a Jew. They don't think of Jesus and Mary as Jewish. But me? I'm still a Jew. And they're right. I am. Catholics are a queer lot—I've never really gotten used to them. I admire their, our, faith, adopted it in fact, but I wish they loved learning more, as they loved it in the High Middle Ages, loved science and art more, like our brother Aristarchus here, just as they loved them in the age of the great Giotto and Roger Bacon and the monk Copernicus and the great Galileo; like Moses Maimonides and Einstein; like the monk Gregor Mendel. We are a church of sinners, yes, but can't sinners love science and art?

But the two, Jew and Catholic, are inextricably attached to each other, like Siamese twins at the umbilicus, whether they like it or not, and they both detest it, until the end of earth time.

I believe that we have the promise of God and his son that he, Jesus Christ, having come once to save us from the death of SELF in search of itSELF without any other SELF, will also come again at the end of the world. We also have his promise that the Church will endure until the end of the world.

Now, it is also the case that I have no reason to believe that the Holy Father or a single bishop has survived the holocaust. As Dr. Jane Smith recently told me, jokingly but more seriously than she knew, I may very well be the Pope. That is to say, as an abbot, I have the episcopal power of consecrating priests. And if there are no bishops left and no Pope left, guess who that leaves. As abbot, I am in the apostolic succession, the direct line of laying on hands which goes back to Christ himself.

As Pope, my first act will be to revive the University of Notre Dame around a nucleus of Jewish scientists whom I shall lure from Israel. The Catholic Church is responsible for the birth of science in the West, but it got too rich, got distracted by family quarrels, and dropped the ball, which the Jews picked up.

Are you getting the point, Captain? I may be the only man left on earth who can consecrate priests. The only candidates for the priesthood I can see, not counting my little malformed innocents, are these boys, your sons, Krishna, Vishnu, Siddhartha, Oppie, Carl Jung, Chomsky, and John. Whether or not one or another chooses to become a priest is his business and God's business, but it is my business to be around, to stay here in case the human race survives and needs priests.

And if it is the end, it is still my obligation to remain, because the Church will survive until the end of earth time and until Christ himself comes, and so, if I'm the putative head of the Church, as putative head I stay.

My proposal: Will your craft fly like an airplane? Yes? Can you land it anywhere? Yes? Like a helicopter? Yes? Very well.

I propose a variant of Dr. Jane Smith's proposal. I propose that you fly Dr. Jane Smith and the children and my odd little brood here and my two monks, yourself, and me, and whoever else wants to go, to Lost Cove, Tennessee.

There, as Dr. Jane Smith and I have reason to believe, the residual radiation is not so bad, that under the blue haze of the Smoky Mountains, the ultraviolet flare may not be excessive, and that your beautiful children may remain fertile.

Accordingly, I propose to you, Captain, that you accede to Dr. Jane Smith's wish that I marry the two of you properly —your marriage in space by yourself is canonically suspect to say the least—and that I baptize the children in Lost Cove Creek.

I wish to come with you for one reason—otherwise, I would rather remain here in my beloved Utah and be let alone and die in peace—but I am obliged to be present to serve the survivors as priest and ordain as priest any one of them who might wish to become a priest, and to await the coming of the Lord if it is the end. I'd as soon wait for him here, but what can you do? Veh.

Why should you of Copernicus 4 believe any of these things, which must surely seem preposterous to you? The only reason, from your point of view, is that you have no choice. You know now that if what I say is not true, you are like the gentiles Paul spoke of: a stranger to every covenant, with no promise to hope for, with the world about you and no God. You are stuck with yourselves, ghost selves, which will never become selves. You are stuck with each other and you will never know how to love each other. Even if you succeed, you and your progeny will go to Europa and roam the galaxy, lost in the Cosmos forever.

I agree with Dr. Jones: we should leave as soon as possible —but for Tennessee, not for Europa.

Question: If you were the captain, which of the two proposals would you accept? or would you accept neither? Do you have a better idea?

(*a*) I'd go with Aristarchus Jones and the others to New Ionia.

(*b*) I'd marry Dr. Jane Smith and take her and the children to Lost Cove, Tennessee.

(*c*) I'd go to Qumran and fight with the Israelis.

(*d*) I'd go to Jordan and fight with the Arabs.

(*e*) I'd drop the abbot and Jane Smith in Tennessee, send the children to Europa with Jones and Tiffany, leaving me and Kimberly to take our chances in Uxmal.

(*f*) I'd take no chances. I'd cover all bets, even the million-to-one shot that there might be something to Abbot Liebowitz's preposterous claim. I'd go with him and Jane and the children to Lost Cove, Tennessee, wait for whatever he's waiting for, monitor my sperm count—yet keep Copernicus 4 fueled and ready to go. (This, roughly, was Dr. Jane Smith's response, in a rather vulgar aside to the Captain, after hearing the abbot's proposal, in which she lapsed into a dialect of her Southern Methodist origins: "Well, why not? Who knows? The whole thing is preposterous, of course: two niggers and a Jew claiming to be Roman Catholics, a Jewish pope and two black monks. Popery and monkery in the middle of nowhere. But what have we got to lose? They're

Christians, after all. I'll go along with it, especially the marriage ceremony and the baptism.")

(g) Other (specify).

(CHECK ONE)

Thought Experiment: An experiment in shifting one's perspective toward the end of determining the relative preposterousness of modern Cartesian consciousness vis-à-vis the preposterousness of Judaeo-Christianity—that is, whether they are two
unrelated preposterousnesses or whether one preposterousness is a function of another, i.e., whether Judaeo-Christianity
is preposterous from the point of view of the modern scientific consciousness precisely to the degree that the latter has
elevated itself from a method of knowing secondary causes
to an all-construing quasi-religious view of the world—
whether, in fact, the preposterousness of Judaeo-Christianity
is not in fact an index of the preposterousness of the age.

Play the following game. Adopt the following perspective: the point of view of Aristarchus Jones (little or no
effort is required of you if you are a creature of the age, that
is, a rational, intelligent, well-educated, objective-minded
denizen of the twentieth century, reasonably well versed in
the sciences and the arts; we are all Aristarchus Jones):

Judaeo-Christianity is indeed a preposterous religion, far
less compatible with the modern scientific temper than, say,
Buddhism or Brahmanism.

Judaism, to begin with, is a preposterous religion. It proposes as a serious claim to truth and for our belief that a
God exists as a spirit separate from us, that he made the
Cosmos from nothing, that he made man, a creature of body
and spirit, that man suffered a fall or catastrophe, and that as
a consequence God entered into a unique covenant with one
of the most insignificant tribes on one of the most insignifi-

cant planets of one of the most insignificant of the 100 billion stars of one of the billions and billions of galaxies of the Cosmos.

Protestant Christianity is even more preposterous than Judaism. It proposes not only all of the above but further, that God himself, the God of the entire Cosmos, appeared as a man, one man and no other, at a certain time and a certain place in history, that he came to save us from our sins, that he was killed, lay in a tomb for three days, and was raised from the dead, and that the salvation of man depends on his hearing the news of this event and believing it!

Catholic Christianity is the most preposterous of the three. It proposes, not only all of the above, but also that the man-god founded a church, appointed as its first head a likable but pusillanimous person, like himself a Jew, the most fallible of his friends, gave him and his successors the power to loose and to bind, required of his followers that they eat his body and drink his blood in order to have life in them, empowered his priests to change bread and wine into his body and blood, and vowed to protect this institution until the end of time. At which time he promised to return.

Second Perspective: Now the game requires that you make a 180-degree shift of point of view from the standard objective view of the Cosmos to a point of view from which you can see the self viewing the Cosmos.

From this new perspective, it can be seen at once that the objective consciousness of the present age is also preposterous.

The earth-self observing the Cosmos and trying to understand the Cosmos by scientific principles from which its self is excluded is, beyond doubt, the strangest phenomenon in all of the Cosmos, far stranger than the Ring Nebula in Lyra.

It, the self, is in fact the only alien in the entire Cosmos.

The modern objective consciousness will go to any length to prove that it is not unique in the Cosmos, and by this very effort establishes its own uniqueness. Name another entity in the Cosmos which tries to prove it is not unique.

The earth-self seeks to understand the Cosmos overtly according to scientific principles while covertly exempting itself from the same understanding. The end of this enterprise is that the self understands the mechanism of the Cosmos but by the same motion places itself outside the Cosmos, an alien, a ghost, outside a vast machinery to which it is denied entry.

Are these two preposterousnesses commensurate or incommensurate, related in direct proportion or unrelated?

That is to say, which of these two propositions is correct?

(1) As time goes on and our science and technology advance and our knowledge of the Cosmos expands, the Judaeo-Christian claim becomes ever more preposterous, anachronistic, and, not to mince words, simply unbelievable.

(2) As time goes on and our science and technology advance and our knowledge of the Cosmos expands, the gap between our knowledge of the Cosmos and our knowledge of ourselves widens and we become ever more alien to the very Cosmos we understand, and our predicament ever more extreme, so that in the end it is precisely this preposterous remedy, it and no other, which is specified by the preposterous predicament of the human self as its sole remedy.

(CHECK ONE)

A new law of the Cosmos, applicable only to the recently appeared triadic creature: If you're a big enough fool to climb a tree and like a cat refuse to come down, then someone who loves you has to make as big a fool of himself to rescue you.

A computer printout of the theoretically ideal convert to Christianity at the end of the twentieth century:

A European who is nationally at the greatest remove from historic Christianity, yet retaining, nevertheless, a faint recollection of Christianity

A person at a remove from the van of scientific research, the laboratory, yet informed by a massive secondhand knowledge of science, the textbook

A person who, feeling himself curiously depressed despite the benefits of science and technology, despite the highest standard of living in Europe, finds solace in the twentieth-century literature of alienation, poetry, art, and film depicting just such a predicament as his

A person old enough to have exhausted the pleasures of the consumption of science as a world view and the pleasures of the consumption of the art of alienation, but not old enough to have become hopeless or to have committed suicide

Sample readout: Sven Olsen, a thirty-five-year-old high-school biology teacher of Örebro, Sweden, who, on the same day, delivered his last lecture of the year on the DNA molecule and saw the last Bergman film, who is therefore suicidal but who retains sufficient curiosity and irony not to do it.

Thought Experiment (II): Imagine yourself in each of these two situations:

(1) You're the captain of the starship.

You go to Europa (New Ionia) with Aristarchus Jones, who also selected twenty young Californians, fifteen females and five males, from Trinity County in the north, which, with its little lost valleys in the Chanchelulla mountains, suffered the least radiation.

The mission is successful. Smooth as a billiard ball and encased in green ice, Europa is crisscrossed by an intricate network of lines, like an old drawing of Mars. These cracks, first observed by Voyager 2, turn out to be rivers of water formed by the mild vulcanism beneath the surface ice.

A colony is established at a place that looks like McMurdo Sound, with pack ice and a low rock ridge and a tundra which flowers with pink and violet lichen in the gentle spring. The atmosphere is rarer than that of the Andes, but, given time for the blood to develop a compensatory polycythemia, and with daily rations of cocaine, life is better than tolerable. No radiation is detected. Sperm counts increase. There is every expectation that the human species will survive.

Here is Aristarchus Jones's famous speech as he surveyed his new home: "A new world! Now I know how the Pilgrim Fathers felt, but unlike the Pilgrims, we left the old world and the old beliefs behind. Free at last! Free at last! No thanks to God, free at last! No irate God, no irate Jews, no irate Christians, no irate Moslems, only liberated loving selves. Now we shall show the Cosmos how to live in peace and freedom. My friends, let us begin by learning to know ourselves, for only by knowing our interior gods and demons can we exorcise them. Our first group session in self-knowledge will be held tomorrow morning. Now let's get to work."

Years pass. Twenty pregnancies occur, and seventeen live normal births. Earth plants, fish, and seals flourish. A peaceful agricultural-fishing society is formed. The colony is operated on the principles of Skinner's Walden II modified by Jungian self-analysis, with suitable rewards for friendly social behavior and punishment, even exile, for aggressive, jealous, hostile, solitary, mystical, or other antisocial behavior. Daily *dewalis* (from the Hindu) are held in a kind of kiva where a dried lichen remarkably like the earth's fruticose *Rocellae* is smoked, inducing a mild euphoria. Larger festivals with dancing and revelry are scheduled for the solstices and equinoxes of the Jovian year.

The Captain, now a sixty-five-year-old man, sits against a rock outside his cave, taking the mild summer sun. The green sky is half filled by the huge northern hemisphere of Jupiter.

He is reading a tattered copy of *Henry IV*. A laser recorder plays for perhaps the seven hundredth time Mozart's fourteenth string quartet. Two young women, Candace and Rima, attend him, each lither and more lovely than Kimberly and Tiffany in their prime. One brings him kelp wine. The other anoints him with seal oil. Dr. Jane Smith, fifty-six, sulks in her cave, knowing quite well she would not be allowed to sulk outside.

Candace refills his glass and, giving him a backward glance, takes a step toward her cave. "Could we? That is to say, when?" she asks and adds: "We have an hour before group."

"Oh, very well." He rises stiffly, closing the book on Mistress Quickly and Prince Hal but picking up the Mozart. Rima's fingers tighten angrily on his trapezius muscle. He winces. "But not without Rima," he tells Candace.

Group is a daily exercise, in assemblages of ten, of self-criticism and honest appraisal of others. The only rule is honesty, absolute honesty. No more lies, no more self-deception, no more secrecy, no more guilt, no more shame. From Aristarchus's own Little Green Book, the aphorism: "The new race will spring from the corpse of the old guilt."

The Captain sighs. He alone of the colonists of the new Ionia is somewhat ironical. Getting rid of guilt is one thing. But he doesn't look forward to the mea culpas and denunciations of the group. It reminds him too much of an AA meeting.

He takes another swig of kelp wine and another look at Candace's behind. Some things don't change.

"Very well," he says again, taking each girl by the hand, the recorder under his arm still playing Mozart.

The three go inside his cave, which is filled with the orange light of Jupiter like a Halloween pumpkin.

(2) You're the Captain.

You choose to go to Tennessee with Abbot Liebowitz. The colony settles in a pleasant mountain valley. You also sleep in a cave, Lost Cove cave, to reduce exposure to radiation, which is still considerable. Sperm counts vary.

Yet the children seem happy and grow strong. Even the misbegotten do well, ramble up and down mountainsides where in fact they are not much different from the local inbred covites.

You grow wild maize, collards, and trap rabbits, wild pigs, and quail, eat grits and sausage and side meat. Every day you watch ironically yet not without affection as the old abbot and his two black priests, black faces and black robes, the blackest blacks in the South, sing the Divine Office in a quavering chant which sounds more Jewish than Latin, and celebrate Mass with corn bread and scuppernong wine, raise a golden chalice, the abbot's only souvenir of Utah. The altar is a slab of limestone, as rough as Stonehenge, fallen across the mouth of the cave, which had no doubt served as a table for the survivors of the last war.

Years pass. The Captain, now sixty-five, sits outside the entrance of Lost Cove cave, where Confederates holed up and made gunpowder some six hundred years earlier.

It is October. The sourwood and sassafras are turning, the leaves speckled in scarlet.

The colony has grown to some two hundred souls, both from successful pregnancies—Dr. Jane had been delivered of two more offspring, two boys, Robert E. Lee Schuyler and John Wesley Schuyler—and from an admixture of locals, strays, wanderers, refugees from the old Northeast. Mostly they are Southerners, white Celtic and Anglo-Saxon, and blacks, with a sprinkling of Hispanics, Jews, and Northern ethnics.

The Captain has formed the habit of sitting on the hillside above the cave, a warm place fragrant with rabbit tobacco and scuppernong and the pine-winey light. It is a favorite meeting place on Sunday mornings of the unbelievers—non-churchgoers and dissidents of one sort and another—while the tiny congregations of Catholics and Protestants hold services. There is even talk of a temple, but the five Jews, one orthodox, one reformed, one conservative, one humanist, and one Yemenite Israeli, cannot get together.

The Captain, two covites (mountain men still wearing bib overalls in the old style), two ex-Atlantans (middle-management types from high-tech industries), three fem-libbers (including Kimberly) who are sick and tired of both the male-dominated space age and the male-dominated clergy, a few twenty-sixth-century hippies, vagabonds from God knows where—gather companionably while the old abbot celebrates Mass below with his two young servers. They, the servers, are white, none other than Siddhartha and Carl Jung, each of whom has already received minor orders. The two black monks are gone. Amos died. Andy discovered his roots in nearby Alabama, resigned his priesthood, and joined the Shiloh Baptist church, a tiny black Baptist community.

"Why don't you come to Mass?" asked Dr. Jane Smith.

"My cathedral is the blue sky. My communion is with my good friends," replied the Captain.

"Bull," said Dr. Jane Smith.

One of the covites, Jason McBee, produces a fruit jar of corn whiskey, by no means the white-lightning of the old bootleggers, but a mellow-gold confection, aged in the wood, smooth as honey, and fiery as the October sun. The Captain takes a long pull.

"Ah," he says.

The "heathen," as they call themselves, begin their usual good-natured bickering, mostly about political and agricultural subjects—whether to start a corn co-op, what to do about a rumored Celtic enclave across the old Carolina line, a growing community with a reputation for violence and snake-handling.

Indeed, one of the covites, the stranger with Jason McBee, has come from Carolina as a kind of emissary. He allows that he wishes to shake their hands in friendship. He does. They drink. The mountain men hunker down. The others sit down. The Carolinian has come to propose a political alliance.

An alliance of whom against whom? the Captain wants to know.

Of us against them.

Who's us?

I'm talking about us rat cheer.

You mean us white folks?

You got it.

No blacks?

No way.

Jews?

We're talking Caucasian. Look at them over there, he says, nodding toward the five Jews.

What about them?

They're conspiring.

Conspiring? Conspiring to do what?

Take over.

They're not conspiring. They're arguing. How about the Catholics down there?

We're talking American. No foreign potentates.

America? What America? There is no America.

Us. American and Christian.

I see. The Captain takes another drink from Jason McBee's

fruit jar and seems to fall into deep thought. Then he begins to laugh.

The others look at him in astonishment. When he catches sight of their faces, he laughs all the harder.

Presently Jason McBee asks him: What you laughing at, Captain?

Nothing much, says the Captain. I was just thinking: Jesus Christ, here we go again.

Below, the old abbot, now withered as a stick, turns from the altar to face the people.

ABBOT: Lord, have mercy on us.

PEOPLE: Christ, have mercy on us.

ABBOT: Lord, have mercy on us.

One of the hippies on the hillside shakes his head. I never did like Sunday, he says. "Sunday mornin' comin' down." Softly he sings an old twentieth-century song:

> On the Sunday morning sidewalks
> Wishing, Lord, that I was stoned
> Makes a body feel alone
> And there's nothing short of dying
> Half as lonesome as the sound
> On the sleeping city sidewalks
> Sunday mornin' comin' down.

Let's move on, he says to his comrades. They do.

The Captain rises creakily, takes a pull of the golden liquor. "I got to get back to the cabin," he says to no one in particular. "Jane will be looking for me. I got a pig in my smoker. I use pecan for smoking. Beats hickory."

One day, in New Ionia or Tennessee, as the case may be, a message is received on the Copernicus antenna, evidently sent many times, for, after it was recorded, it was repeated again and again. Its source was nothing else than an ETI (extraterrestrial intelligence), the first after all these hundreds of years of monitoring.

Question: Where would you rather be when the message is received—
    (1) Tennessee?
    (2) New Ionia?

The Message:

Message to Star: G2V, r = 9.844 kpc, o = 00°05′24″, o = 206°28′49″ (our sun)

Planets: a = 1.5 × 10¹³ cm, M = 6 × 10²⁷ g, R = 6.4 × 10⁸ cm, p = 8.6 × 10⁴, p = 3.2 × 10⁷ s (the inner planets of the solar system)

Repeat. Do you read? Do you read? Are you in trouble? How did you get in trouble? If you are in trouble, have you sought help? If you did, did help come? If it did, did you accept it? Are you out of trouble? What is the character of your consciousness? Are you conscious? Do you have a self? Do you know who you are? Do you know what you are doing? Do you love? Do you know how to love? Are you loved? Do you hate? Do you read me? Come back. Repeat. Come back. Come back. Come back.

(CHECK ONE)